Front Lines

Becoming an Effective Sports Chaplain or Character Coach

Roger D. Lipe

FRONT LINES

Cross Training Publishing
www.crosstrainingpublishing.com
(308) 293-3891

ISBN: 978-1-952222-02-3

ACKNOWLEDGEMENTS

I would like to acknowledge the following people and groups for their contributions to this book.

Thanks to my wife, Sharon Lipe, for her unwavering support of my pursuit of God's purposes for my life.

Thanks to Saluki Athletics at Southern Illinois University in Carbondale. I am thankful for the administrators, coaches, support staff, and student-athletes who have welcomed my service and have endured my mistakes for twenty-six years.

Thanks to Fred Bishop of No Greater Love Ministries. Fred has been a leader, instructor, intercessor, mentor, and friend for several decades. I am forever in his debt.

Thank you to my colleagues from the Fellowship of Christian Athletes. My service as a sports chaplain has been tremendously enhanced by sharing stories, best practices, successes, and failures with my FCA teammates.

Thanks to my colleagues from the Global Sports Chaplaincy Association, learning from and contributing to sports chaplaincy leaders from around the world is immeasurably valuable to me.

Thanks to my daughter-in-law Jenn Lipe for her assistance in editing the book, and to Dan Bishop and Josh Franklin for the title and subtitle, respectively.

Comments on Front Lines

"This book is arguably the most practical and insightful offering on Sport Chaplaincy on the market. Due to Roger's long involvement at the coal-face of Sport Chaplaincy and his willingness and openness to engage academically with the topic, the sections of this book are filled with clear and helpful advice on how to become, and to be, a an effective minister for Christ in the domain of sport."

Dr Nick J. Watson, Chief Operating Officer, Archbishop of York Youth Trust and former Associate Professor, Sport and Social Justice, York St. John University, UK

"Drawing upon years of faithful service and practice wisdom, this book comprises a candid and highly informative resource which chaplains and mentors across any number of sports will find invaluable."

Dr. Andrew Parker, Director at Andrew Parker Consulting Ltd. and former Professor of Sport and Christian Outreach at the University of Gloucestershire, UK

"Sport chaplains enter a world of relative fame, competing agendas, and raw emotion. The role requires near constant self-reflection and discernment for understanding the sport culture and serving the people involved.

In Front Lines, Roger Lipe shares his practiced wisdom from decades of sport chaplaincy in accessible, bite-sized sections each equally profound and practical. From start to finish, this book unpacks the how questions of sport chaplaincy while always remaining tethered to the important question of why, offering an invaluable and authentic resource for people in sports ministry and beyond."

Dr. Brian Bolt, Professor, Dean of Education, Calvin University, Grand Rapids, Michigan, USA

"If you are one either on the front lines of sports chaplaincy, or in the midst of considering a call to join, Roger Lipe's 20+ years of ministry experience and distilled here in these pages, Front Lines, will help ready you and mature you for the work ahead that God has for you."

Rev Brad Kenney, Founder/Director, Soccer Chaplains United, Lead Volunteer Chaplain, Colorado Rapids, USA

CONTENTS

INTRODUCTION

Front Lines

Becoming an Effective Sports Chaplain
or Character Coach

In July of 1994 I walked into the offices of Saluki Football on the campus of Southern Illinois University in Carbondale, Illinois. I went in to welcome the new thirty-four year old head coach for Saluki Football, Shawn Watson, back to campus. He had played here, had started his coaching career, and had just arrived on campus with a mountainous challenge and modest resources.

During our conversation I offered to help him in any way I could, and he said, "When I played here we had team chaplain. Would you do that for me?" I agreed to do it, we prayed together, and I walked out of the office without one solitary idea of what to do.

I walked down the hall to see our athletic director, Jim Hart. Jim had played eighteen years in the National Football League and I hoped he would have some ideas for me. He provided two memories of his chaplain while with the St. Louis Cardinals, Walt Enoch.

Those simple lessons from Walt were very helpful, but I had a lot to learn. The contents of this book are the things I wish I had known when I first started. More than twenty-five years of experiences and insights are contained herein. I hope they serve you well as you serve the men and women of sport in your community.

Roger D. Lipe

Sports Chaplaincy Essentials:
Character Qualities

Persistence

Among the most important qualities for sport chaplains and sport mentors is to be persistent.

Dictionary.com says that to persist is:

1. to continue steadfastly or firmly in some state, purpose, course of action, or the like, especially in spite of opposition, remonstrance, etc.

2. to last or endure tenaciously.

Persistence is important when relationships are slow to develop. It could take months or years for relationships of trust to develop to the point where we are allowed access to the coach or player's heart. One much endure tenaciously to win the right to hear their hearts and to be heard.

Persistence is important when results are vague or slow in arriving. If we will continue steadfastly in our commitment to the people and in our commitment to the right way to serve, we can handle it if we don't see the results we expect or if they don't arrive in the time we have anticipated or promised.

Persistence is indispensable when we encounter opposition. To be firm in our purpose and course of action is critical when we know we're doing the right thing, for the right reason, with the right people. We will surely be opposed at some point. Persistence will enable us to stay on course rather than veer away from our central purposes.

I would challenge us all to hold tightly to the principles

of ministry which guide our work, to persist strongly on the course of action which leads to the fulfillment of our calling and to endure tenaciously in the face of opposition, from without or within.

Discernment

Discernment—"the trait of judging wisely and objectively."

For decades I have heard people say things like, "Don't judge him. Don't be too quick to make judgments. We're in no position to judge." However, every day we desperately need the trait of judging wisely and objectively in order to serve the people of sport well.

We need discernment to decide if something is genuine or artificial? Was that a genuine or artificial apology to his teammates? Is that coach being genuine or artificial in his statements about matters of faith?

Is this course of action being proposed wise or foolish? A discerning person can see the end result well before it arrives. He or she can help avoid the consequences of a poor decision by asking good questions or reframing the discussion with insight.

Is this person an ally or an enemy? A discerning person can see through the smoke screens of deception, flattery and inflated resumes. A person of discernment can be of tremendous value to an organization in the recruiting, hiring and development process.

Is he or she real or simply posing? Discernment helps us see the true nature of a person more clearly. The discerning person can see through the posing of the player who says what he thinks the coach wants to hear. She can hear the conviction and purity of heart of a young lady whose motivations are pure.

Should we commit to this decision or wait for a while?

Pull the trigger or no? Move or stay? Hire or not? Fire this person or be patient with him? The discerning of heart seem to have an intuitive sense of timing and then confidence with their decisions, long before the fruit of the decision is visible to everyone else.

If you are a person of discernment serving as a Sport Chaplain or Sport Mentor, you are of immeasurable value. When asked for your thoughts on a matter requiring discernment, share your thoughts freely and confidently. If they ask your opinion, you are free to share the wisdom God has given you. It's precisely because you are trusted and are perceived to be discerning that the question is asked. Ask the Lord Jesus for an extra measure of discernment and then employ it well in serving the people of sport as they make important decisions.

Intuition

Most of us who are male are assumed to be lacking intuition. All my life I've heard about "women's intuition" and I've seen it in action in my mother, my wife, friends, coworkers and many others. I certainly know my wife to be more intuitive than me and I trust her intuition because her hunches are usually more on target than my logical, overly analyzed view of people and situations. Related to intuition and its value for ministry in sport, our female colleagues seem to have a head start on their brothers.

However, we who possess X and Y chromosomes and serve as sport chaplains or sport mentors may be some of the most intuitive people walking the planet. Many of us act on hunches much more often than we follow a carefully planned agenda. Most of us have more phone numbers than appointments in our mobile phones. We are often more people oriented than task oriented. We act on our gut, follow hunches, take chances which often don't make sense and will take great risks for those we love and serve.

In fact, the lack of documentation about sports chaplaincy is a strong indicator of how most of us do our work intuitively rather than strategically. Strategically thinking people write outlines and schedules. Intuitive people just do what seems right and trust God with the results. Check out Malcolm Gladwell's book, "Blink" for some insight about how often one's intuitive hunch is correct and how much we can trust our intuition.

Intuition is an important gift and should be trusted in situations like:

· Which of the dozens of players should I speak with today?

· I have a feeling that _____ is bothered by something, should I speak to him?

· _____ seems grieved, should I offer my support?

· That coach may be fired soon; should I give him a call?

· I heard that _____ is having surgery today; should I go by the hospital or back to the office?

· Coach _____ seems to be under a lot of pressure; should I send her a text message?

· There's something about this player which seems a little off; should I ask her if everything's okay?

· About what should I speak at this week's chapel?

· What is the condition of this player's heart? What would God say to him?

· What would encourage Coach _____'s heart in this trying season?

· _____ just came across my mind; should I contact her?

· I can't get _____ off my mind today; should I go see him?

· My heart is broken for _____. Lord; what do You want me to say to her?

As one who is often distrustful of intuitive thoughts, may I challenge you to take some risks? Last Thursday I was talking with a colleague, and he mentioned a coach who is our mutual friend. I asked about our friend's job security, given the long losing streak he was enduring, and was asked to give him a call. I made time the next day, researched the phone number and called, only to reach his voice mail.

Undeterred, I left the same message on the voice mail that I would have delivered directly to his ear. I ended the call feeling my effort was weak and wondering at its value. Monday afternoon I learned that my friend was fired that morning. I was so glad that I had made the call, that I had followed my hunch and my friend's urging.

Bottom line: let your gift of intuition work for you and for those whom you serve. Take some risks, even if they seem illogical to you. You may be making the call, the visit, text message or the email at just the right time and your words could be as valuable as apples of gold in settings of silver (Proverbs 25:11).

Confidence

Let's consider another of the essential qualities for effective service as a sports chaplain or mentor. Confidence is a most important characteristic for such service as we live in a culture of people who vacillate between arrogance and humiliation depending upon their last performance. In either case, we must act confidently to be of value to their growing lives in sport and faith.

We need confidence when we walk into uncomfortable situations. If we're well prepared and confident in our training, we can step into the coach's office after a crushing defeat knowing we can serve the team well. To be of assistance with questions related to discipline of a player or staff member, or to help those we serve deal with illness, disease, injury and even death requires a confidence which is born of a liberated heart, a pure conscience and a humble attitude.

Confidence is important to help us know where we fit. If we're in a sport setting, and confidence wells up within us, we feel like we fit in here, we relax and we're free to be our best.

Confidence is a byproduct of our being genuine in our roles with the players, coaches, teams and support staff. They perceive that we're not playing a role. We're not pretending or posing as those who say they want to serve, but are secretly just seeking access to the players and "off limits" areas.

Confidence is indispensable when we walk into hospital rooms where the coach is receiving chemotherapy. It's of immeasurable value when we step into the uncertain world of the emergency room. We're immediately perceived to have it or to be lacking it when we step onto the field, pitch, floor, ice or the court.

Let's build our confidence upon the unchanging nature of Christ's love, grace and mercy toward us. Let's find it more in our Lord's calling upon or lives than in our background, experience, education or affiliations. Let a genuine confidence grow in your heart, show on your countenance and flow from your mouth as you extravagantly love the men and women of sport.

Empathy

There are some qualities which enable sports chaplains and sports mentors to be most effective in their work with coaches and competitors. One of those is empathy. Empathy is the ability to see situations from another's point of view, to even feel what the other is feeling. Empathy shapes our attitudes and aligns our hearts and emotions to be most effective at communicating God's heart in any given situation.

For those of us in sports ministry, we need empathy to properly engage people's hearts. In failure, empathy helps me to feel the pain along with the player or coach. In success, empathy allows me to rejoice with them and to share their joy. In frustration, empathy keeps me from saying something foolish or acting as if their frustration is unwarranted or silly. In pain, empathy keeps me from communicating in trite clichés. In loss, empathy keeps me from saying, "It's just a game," thus creating distance and distrust with the coaches and players.

Empathy is dangerous and brings about significant emotional and mental risks. It's easier and safer to stay aloof and untouched by the pain, frustration, loss and even the exhilaration of success. To remain untouched by these emotions limits our connection with those we serve. To risk the dangers of empathy also brings with it the reward of deep connection, trust and genuine community with our friends in sport.

The challenge for today is to take the risks to empathize with the men and women of sport in your circle of influence.

Give them your heart and trust the Lord to sustain you and to speak through you in the process.

Loyalty

My wife, Sharon, and my mentor, Fred Bishop, are among the most fiercely loyal people I've ever met. They refuse to quit on the people to whom they're committed under any circumstances. They will consistently support their friends, teammates and colleagues when they fail, when they are under intense criticism and even when they display poor character. Such loyalty is an admirable trait in a spouse, a mentor and a friend and is an indispensable characteristic in a sport chaplain or sport mentor.

According to dictionary.com, to be loyal is "to be faithful to one's oath, commitments, or obligations: to be loyal to a vow." We certainly expect faithfulness to one's wedding vows and look for it among teammates, but it is often a rare commodity among the people of sport. The sports media are full of stories of competitive failure, moral failure and character issues among coaches and competitors. Coaches who are fired for too few wins, players who are suspended for doping, team officials who are found to have ties to gambling interests, competitors who speak foolishly during interviews and thus incur the wrath of their club or league and other instances put us who serve them in difficult situations and leave us with hard questions to be asked.

Hard questions which test our loyalty:
· How shall I relate to the coach who was just fired for lack of success?
· What should I say to our coach who was exposed in a sex scandal?
· Our best player was just suspended for a violation of team

rules. How shall I approach him?

· What is my responsibility toward the coach who was just "outed" and identified as a lesbian?

· After months of bitter conflict, our head coach resigned. Should I seek him out or just let him go?

· One of our committed Christian players was just benched for poor performance. How shall I encourage her?

These and similar situations often stretch to the limit the loyalty of our hearts. We often find the faithfulness we want to give to our friends and teammates in conflict with our drive for success, our taste for popularity and our desire for status. Let's think this matter through and let the Spirit of Christ guide our hearts to make wise decisions.

We must display loyalty to those we serve in sports:

· On their way down as well as on their way up.

· When they lose as well as when they win.

· When they endure criticism by the media as well as when they're the media darlings.

· When they are dead wrong, foolish and out of line as well as when they are wise and totally in the right.

Let's be the ones in sport who are loyal, faithful and consistent. There are plenty of people who will be capricious, politically expedient and adrift on the fickle seas of public opinion.

Highly Committed, but Irreligious

While preparing for a pre-game meal and chapel talk one day, an assistant women's basketball coach commented to me, "You're not like most of the religious people I've known." I smiled and replied, "Good. I don't intend to be religious. I would prefer to be highly committed to Christ, but rather irreligious." She said, "That's interesting." My reflexive comment to my friend was true and heart-felt and I'm still happy with it.

I'd like to explore the difference between being "religious" and being "highly committed to Christ." Religious people carry the external trappings of Christianity as their defining marks. Highly committed Christians carry their commitment to Jesus internally as their defining characteristic and allow that commitment to find external expression in numerous, often less religious ways. Some examples of each may help us see the difference.

Religious people speak with each other in clichés and the King James language they learn at church. Highly committed believers in Jesus are free to speak in the language of the subculture in which they are serving Him; in our case, that is the language of sport. Religious people would rather sit in judgment over people whose lifestyles don't fit their standards. Highly committed Christian men and women demonstrate love and commitment to those they serve without respect to their lifestyles, wise or foolish. Their grasp of their own wickedness of heart and the weakness of their own flesh keeps judgmental attitudes at bay.

I don't shun the sinful or cluck my tongue at foolish

speech. I don't Tebow because it's trendy nor do I repeat or retweet every syllable uttered by John Piper (insert the name of any other celebrity preacher) as if it were holy writ. I don't pretend that attending my local church is the answer to everyone's social ills and that if they simply walk through the door all their problems will be solved. I don't counsel new believers in Jesus to shun their former circle of friends and teammates in order to adopt a more suitable set of friends who won't pollute their lives with wickedness. I don't wear WWJD bracelets and I haven't burned my secular music recordings (Gasp!). I don't go to trendy "Christian films" which are simply gospel tracts on celluloid. I'm bored with the passionless music poured out by contemporary Christian music stations and I'm repulsed by Southern Gospel music. I prefer reading Seth Godin and Malcom Gladwell to Max Lucado and Joel Osteen.

This distaste for "religious" things and preference for "heartfelt commitment" often leads to my being misunderstood by others in the Church. I'm fine with that. I rather enjoy the questions asked of me about such things; the question asked by the assistant basketball coach being emblematic of such questions and the conversations which normally follow. Please take the risk of being misunderstood and questioned about your lack of religiousness in favor of a genuine, passionate expression of your love for the Lord Jesus. It's worth it and we're much less boring people with whom to interact.

Watch Your Attitude

Across more than twenty years of serving as a sports chaplain, the three primary, universal factors that I have found to build an effective ministry are: relationships, attitudes, and presence. I would like to make some simple and direct comments regarding attitudes and how they can either enhance or diminish our service.

Be a servant, not a big shot. Serve purposefully. Do the menial tasks that need to be done in service of others. People will notice, and they will respect your attitude.

Seek permission, not forgiveness. Ask for parameters. Understand your boundaries. To overstep your bounds communicates the wrong attitude.

Be thankful, out loud. Express thankfulness to those who give you access to their sporting programs in person, via text message, on paper, however you can.

Talk in terms of "responsibility and privilege" rather than "rights." An entitled attitude is repulsive to sportspeople, especially coaches. Avoid it at all costs.

A low public profile is to be preferred over media darling. Be less interested in being a public figure, and more in being an essential part of the team's life.

Deflect praise quickly. As you do well and others praise you for what you have done, be sure to direct that praise to God and to those with whom you serve.

Beware of reflected glory. If your team is excelling, beware the allure of fame, accolades, and public adoration. It's fun, but it can be a snare to your soul.

Remember that your contributions do not appear on the

scoreboard or stat sheets. Don't be fooled into thinking that your inspirational talk directly contributed to a victory.

Love extravagantly—it's really hard to fail if this is your number one goal.

Serve selflessly—to do this faithfully almost always keeps one's attitude in order.

Please shape your attitude in ways that are reflective of Christ Jesus' as described in Philippians chapter 2:3-8. "Do nothing from selfishness or empty conceit, but with humility of mind regard one another as more important than yourselves; do not merely look out for your own personal interests, but also for the interests of others. Have this attitude in yourselves which was also in Christ Jesus, who, although He existed in the form of God, did not regard equality with God a thing to be grasped, but emptied Himself, taking the form of a bond-servant, and being made in the likeness of men. Being found in appearance as a man, He humbled Himself by becoming obedient to the point of death, even death on a cross."

Through What Lens
Do You View Sport?

Through what lens do you view sport? I'm not asking how good your seats are for viewing sport at the arena or stadium, rather when you're thinking about sport, is your perspective one from the seats, through a television camera, from the luxury box at the stadium or from the sideline at field/court level? The answer to this question has powerful implications for how one does ministry with people of sport.

If one sees sport through the sports fan's lens he tends to see the players and coaches as celebrities, valuing the spectacle and seeing sport like other forms entertainment. While he seems loyal to the team, paying for expensive seats, wearing team gear and cheering loudly, his experience is as the consumer of the event. The implications for ministry are that celebrities and entertainers often seem rather distant and even unapproachable to fans. That makes for surface level ministry, at best. It also lends itself to using the Christian player as a part of "the show" at Church or we capitalize on her celebrity status for our magazine, our radio or television show, sometimes without respect to the development (or lack of it) of her life in Christ. If you see sport primarily as a fan, be very cautious about your motives as you serve sportspeople.

If one sees sport through the television camera's lens he often values comfort, instant replay, availability of multiple games and slow motion for maximum enjoyment of the game. Sitting in the recliner, remote control in one hand, favorite beverage in the other and bountiful snacks at his side, the arm chair quarterback and coach enjoys the game without any relationship with the sportspeople and sometimes without even relationships with other spectators.

At its worst, this perspective leads the viewer to see the sportspeople like video game characters. They're dehumanized, criticized and stripped of all human dignity when they fail. When they succeed they're lionized, adored and even worshiped as demigods. The implications for ministry are rather obvious. If this is one's view of sport, the first hurdle is to simply deal with the people of sport as human beings and not images on a screen. To connect with and to speak to their hearts is a huge leap if we're accustomed to seeing them as two dimensional characters on our living room TVs. If this is your usual view of sport, get ready to make a huge shift in your thinking before you start serving sportspeople.

If one sees sport through the privileged glass of a luxury box at the stadium or arena, she sees it almost like a chess match. The players seem to be laid out on a game board and they almost appear to be plastic figures moving across the grid. The box's occupants value luxury, prestige, power and influence. The coaches look like the kings and queens of sport, and the players vary in value from bishops to pawns, but they're all subject to the will of the masters in the box. Ministry implications for this viewpoint are severe. From here it's easy to control people, but difficult to care for them. It's easy to influence them, but difficult to inspire them. It's easy to manipulate them, but terribly hard to nurture their lives in Christ. It's not impossible, but immeasurably more difficult to care for the hearts of the players when your voice is muffled and face obscured by the luxury box's glaring glass.

If one sees sport from the sideline or even from the pitch, his or her values are most closely matched with the players and coaches he or she seeks to serve. Those who are privileged to be and pay the cost to be in this position become fully aware that these are real people with real virtues and vices. Their relationships are real, both flawed and flourishing. Their emotions are real, anguish and exhilaration. Their pain is real, emotional and physical. Their exertion of effort is real, not plastic like a chess game, not like a video game electronic image and not rooted in "school spirit" like a fan might think. If one has this perspective and is willing to fully embrace these sportspeople, full of virtues and vices, he or she is in a perfect position to care for, to nurture, to speak to their hearts. If this is your perspective, wrap both arms and your whole heart around the sporting community, and love them with Christ Jesus' sustaining power.

If you are privileged to serve the people of sport as a sports chaplain, as a character coach or as a sports mentor, be mindful of your internal lens on sport. Be diligent to adjust your view to one which most properly serves those for whom you care. Seeing sport through their lens will help you communicate more clearly and connect most directly with their hearts.

Divinely Ruined

A number of years ago, while conversing with my dear friend and ministry partner, David Maragni, he said, "Rog, we have been divinely ruined." My friend's simple phrase really resonated in my soul as it's a spot-on description of what the Lord has done to me. He has ruined me in so many ways that have shaped my view of the world, sport, the Church, and the Kingdom of God.

A few examples of how I am divinely ruined are listed below:

I prefer the sound of sport (cracks of baseballs colliding with bats) to the sounds of music (even U2).

I prefer the smell of ballpark grills or the menthol in a gym to the incense in a cathedral.

I prefer listening to the sounds of a one-hour sports practice to the sounds of my talking anywhere.

I prefer sporting events to motion pictures.

I much prefer sports culture to church culture.

I prefer being on the field, court, or pitch over free, first row field boxes, or luxury suites at the stadium.

I prefer faithfulness over fame.

I prefer walking through international airports over driving my car, anywhere.

I prefer leading a baseball chapel for 10 players in a dugout over speaking to a crowd of hundreds at a church service.

I prefer grace over greed.

I prefer relationships over religious ritual.

I prefer significance over celebrity.

Dave and I, possibly you as well, have been divinely ruined toward God's purposes. He has uniquely wired us to prefer things that make most people tilt their heads and wonder, "What's wrong with them?" We're divinely ruined, in the best possible ways. Let's live freely in our extraordinarily shaped souls.

Sports Chaplaincy Essentials: Identity

Sport and Identity

During a recent FCA Coaches Ministry event, the presenter made an excellent statement regarding the power of sport in cultures. He said that it was a matter of identity and tied it to three specific dynamics in which people find identity.

1. Sport gives people a sense of belonging to something.
2. Sport gives people a cause greater than one's self.
3. Sport gives people a sense of purpose.

That idea immediately resonated with me and I've been thinking about it for the two weeks since I heard it. Let's think about each of these ideas and draw some ministry points from them.

1. Sport gives people a sense of belonging to something. This is certainly the case for the countless young people who come to sport from terribly fractured backgrounds. It's common for them to feel terribly alone since the normal structures to which they could belong are broken. Family, church, community, and other support structures, for them, are either shattered or absent altogether. Some of the things in which they may find this sense of belonging are pernicious: gangs are far too common on the margins of society, and they prey on the lost sense of belonging in young people. Sports teams have been a redemptive factor for generations of young people, providing a sense of family, a set of adults who genuinely care about them, loving nurture

for their young souls, and safety for their entire vulnerable selves. This is even true for sports fans as it's rather common to see middle-aged men wearing ridiculously expensive, "authentic" game jerseys of their favorite teams emblazoned with the name of their favorite player on the back. To identify with the sports team gives these people a sense of belonging to something, even more, something successful and socially prominent. Just watch your social media feeds for posts re: "_____ Nation!!" Many fans find themselves being identified by their favorite sports teams. Many sportspeople wear their team gear in public, away from sporting environments, primarily because their identity is directly tied to their belonging to the team.

    2. Sport gives people a cause greater than one's self. To be a part of a sports team gives people the sense of being caught up in movement. As a part of the team, there are other people working with the individual, there are coaches giving leadership, there is a specific goal at hand that we all strive together to accomplish. The cause, pursuing a victory, building our team, developing our teamwork, and more is the stuff of inspiration and motivation. Many young people move from a sporting experience in video game form, where the individual controls everything, to a genuine sporting experience where he or she is a part of a larger movement of people, and many find it liberating. Others obsess over the loss of control. In either case, they find that sport gives them a sense of being a part of a cause greater than themselves. Sports fans also connect here as they will often see themselves as a part of the team and its cause. You'll hear

fans say, "We won by 14 points yesterday." As if they had anything to do with the victory, they use first person pronouns to describe the event. They feel that they're a part of the cause. A sportsperson's mood, the ones actually engaged in sport, is often directly tied to the results of his or her most recent competition. The success or failure of the cause is felt deeply as the person is so tightly identified with it.

3. Sport gives people a sense of purpose. One of the best things about sport is that it engages all of the sportsperson's life in it. When sport is at its best, body, mind, spirit, and social elements of each person is deeply involved in the pursuit of excellence and a goal. This gives the sportsperson a great sense of purpose. It helps one feel like his or her life matters. We feel like we fit in the world. This is true for the 60 year old team chaplain standing on the sideline of a college football game, chatting with a women's basketball coach at practice, leaning over the rail at a swim meet to encourage a swimmer, or leading a Bible study between batting practice and game time. I have a great sense of purpose in these sporting environments, and there is no place I'd rather be. I believe this is also part of the reason people engage in "fantasy team" leagues and others wager on sporting events. Surely greed and the love of money is a part of it, but some find these activities to provide a personal sense of purpose for each week's NFL game. They don't even follow their favorite teams, they root for the statistical performance of individual players or for the teams on which they bet to achieve relative to the wagered point spread.

Sport can provide a great sense of presence, often wisely for the sportsperson directly involved, but often less than wisely for those living through it vicariously via fantasy teams or gambling on it.

The whole discussion of one's identity being found in sport has to be tempered by the understanding that it is inherently limited and even dangerous. To tie one's sense of identity to an activity that will be ultimately posted on a scoreboard has real problems. It's too flighty and insecure to be healthy. To be identified by the life, death, burial, and resurrection of Christ Jesus, to be found in Him, to be crucified with Him, to be raise up with Him, to be His workmanship, to be His joint heir, is much more secure and much more fulfilling.

May I challenge you as I do myself? First and foremost, rest your identity fully in the personal work of and relationship with Christ. Secondly, find great joy, fulfillment, sorrow, loss, exhilaration, and grief in the daily experiences of sport. The security of the former allows us to take the risks of the latter. It's reasonable for us to find a sense of belonging, a cause bigger than ourselves, and a strong sense of purpose in sport, if it is subjected to the rock solid sense of belonging, cause, and purpose we have as being a child of the Living God. There is no need to reject one to hold to the other. Hold your life in sport loosely, it is fleeting and temporal. Christ Jesus holds your life in Him tightly, it is secure and eternal.

Five Lies of a Sports Chaplain's Identity

In 2019 I saw a tweet that quoted Henri Nouwen's Five lies of identity. It seems that this idea was delivered in a lecture by Henri Nouwen titled, "Who are We?: Exploring our Christian Identity." I had heard some of these articulated by others but was glad to find the original source for these ideas.

Henri Nouwen's Five Lies of Identity:

1) I am what I have.

2) I am what I do.

3) I am what other people say or think of me.

4) I am nothing more than my worst moment.

5) I am nothing less than my best moment.

Five Lies of a Sports Chaplain's or Character Coach's Identity:

1) I am what I have. It's a trap to find one's identity in the privilege he's given, in the prestige she receives by being connected with a team, in the team gear one is given to wear, in the championship rings some are blessed to receive, in the public platform we sometimes perilously ascend, or in the access we are afforded to changing rooms, to sidelines, to the coaches offices and more. Sports Chaplain, what you have does not define you. Most of it can easily be taken away or foolishly forfeited.

2) I am what I do. Serving as a sports chaplain or character coach is what I do, not who I am. To be the confidante to celebrity sportspeople is a responsibility, not a defining characteristic of one's life. To be chaplain to

champions in sport is a privilege, not a personal identity. Any or all these descriptions may be true of what we do, but they are neither primary nor permanent statements of our identity.

3) I am what other people say or think of me. I am not what others may see as a glamourized image, strolling the sidelines of a sports arena. I am not how others' flattery portrays me. I am not defined by my public reputation, good or bad. I am essentially as I am perceived in the poorly informed esteem of my colleagues and friends. Others' opinions, their flattery or criticism, nor any other external assessment of me defines my life.

4) I am nothing more than my worst moment. My lack of poise in a critical moment is not a life defining situation. My absence when I was critically needed does not establish my identity. When I have spoken foolishly, when morally compromised, when exposed by ethical failure, when fired from my role, when publicly accused of wrongdoing, or when nothing I do seems to bear fruit, none of these moments of failure or neglect ultimately define who I am as a person.

5) I am nothing less than my best moment. I am not defined 100% by my highest achievement, by my association with a championship team, by the times when everyone responds well, or when it seems everything we touch flourishes. Our identity cannot be hung on the fleeting memories of our best days. To be defined by our personal highlight videos is simultaneously pitiful and delusional.

Our identity is primarily in Christ. This identity is genuine, secure, and timeless. It's quite natural for us to be lured into believing the lies of identity, as Nouwen lists them. It is critical that we eschew the lies and hold tightly to our identity in Christ Jesus. Lean into these scriptures, and rest in your immutable identity in Christ.

The Sport Chaplain's
Dirty Little Secret

After many years of serving coaches and competitors in various sports and almost as many years of networking with sports chaplains and sport mentors around the USA and the world, I've become convinced that our dirty little secret is that many, if not most, of us are just as performance based in our sense of personal worth as those whom we serve in the world of sport.

We can all see how driven by their last performance our charges are in how they perceive their personal identity, even those who claim a relationship with Christ Jesus. We all hear players say things like, "I'm 7 and 5." That is a direct statement of worth based on wins and losses. They might protest when asked about that, but it's still an indicator of what's really important to them. If we ask, "How are you doing?" many will reply by stating their team's record or their personal statistics rather than anything deeper than their most recent results. I usually get the same sorts of replies from coaches, administrators, fans and even sports chaplains.

For sports chaplains, we usually point to more "spiritual" results. "Eighty-five players came to chapel today." "Fifteen players committed their lives to Christ last week." "Our team has 80% of the players attending Bible study each week." "Ten of the twelve coaches are in our weekly Coaches Bible studies." Honorable results all, but they must not become the basis for our identity or the defining marks of the validity of our ministries. Would I be less valuable to God if five players attended chapel instead of 50? Would Christ be less pleased with me if this year no one committed his life to Christ through my ministry? Am I a failure if no one wants to start a Coaches Bible Study? Is my identity tied directly to my performance of "spiritual tasks?"

Why is this important? If I find my worth and identity in my performance, I will do whatever it takes to get to the desired results. I'll manipulate people to acquire the decisions which validate my ministry. I'll be sure to report the numbers which satisfy those who finance my ministry, even if they're a little exaggerated. I'll choose programs over people, methods over relationships and masses over individuals because they provide the results which define my success and my worth.

If we are to have any hope of being agents of Christ's transforming power in the lives of the people of sport, we must find our worth in our relationship with Him. At the beginning of Jesus' ministry, as He is being baptized by John in the Jordan River, He comes up from the water and hears a voice saying, "You are my Son, whom I love; with you I am well pleased." (Mark 1:11) To this point, Jesus had zero followers. He had performed zero miracles. He had healed zero people. He had raised zero people from the dead. He had accomplished nothing to earn His Father's love and approval. He is pleasing to God the Father because Jesus is His Son. That's all. The relationship was the basis for God's pleasure and approval. Jesus was identified by His relationship with His Father, period. That continued throughout His life on the earth and beyond.

This is pretty easy for me to see because it's very easy for me to fall prey to such a performance based mentality. It is a constant battle to check my attitudes, my values, my priorities, my methods and my relationships to see if they are reflective of a heart which finds its worth in relationship with Christ or if it seems driven by performance and easily defined results. It's very easy to find my emotions and perspective directly reflective of the most recent results of the teams I serve. It is also very easy to find my sense of identity being tied directly to the success or failure of our ministry's most recent events. If you were honest, you'd probably confess the same.

So what shall we do? Let's regularly evaluate our ministries to see how clearly we communicate each one's intrinsic worth to our loving Father. Let's be sure to lead others in ways which value relationships over results. Let's honor faithfulness over success. Let's guard our hearts from the insidious cancer of performance based worth and prefer to live in the freedom and security of knowing we're well pleasing to God through our relationship with Christ Jesus. Having such a secure basis for our own worth will leave us free to serve selflessly and to help others find their own freedom from the burdensome yoke of slavery to performance.

Sports Chaplaincy Essentials:
Values

A "Thumbnail Sketch"
of Sports Chaplaincy

While in St. Petersburg, Russia in 2019, and serving with FCA Eurasia teammates, I was asked to prepare a brief "thumbnail sketch" of what Sports Chaplains do and how they serve. I scratched out a simple five-point outline for sharing with those entirely unacquainted with this form of ministry. That outline is below. I like it and I hope you do also.

1. Sports Chaplains (Character Coaches) are ambassadors for Christ Jesus and His Church in the sporting community.

2. Sports Chaplains (Character Coaches) love extravagantly. We love God. We love the people of sport, at their best and at their worst.

3. Sports Chaplains (Character Coaches) serve selflessly. We serve God. We serve the people of sport, at their best and at their worst.

4. Sports Chaplains (Character Coaches) are invited guests of the sports clubs, the teams, the federations, coaches, competitors, and support staffs they serve.

5. A Sports Chaplain's (Character Coach's) service is built upon these three pillars:

- Relationships
- Attitudes
- Presence

It helps to think about these three in this sequence:

- Be seen.
- Be known.
- Be heard.

Relationships, attitudes, and presence all inform and empower this process.

There it is. Simple but descriptive of the essence of our ministry in sport.

Purpose

Over the last several years more and more people are talking, thinking, and writing about purpose. From Rick Warren's, *The Purpose Driven Life*, and its accompanying market offshoots to any number of websites, podcasts, and blogs, it seems purpose is on everyone's mind. A simple Google search of the word "purpose" leads to this message: "About 3,130,000,000 results."

I have been contemplating how the Lord might express His thoughts about purpose and I took a leisurely stroll through the Bible searching for answers. A sampling of the most direct expressions of purpose are below with some simple remarks on each.

God's purpose:

I cry out to God Most High, to God who will fulfill his purpose for me. Psalms 57:2

For David, after he had served the purpose of God in his own generation, fell asleep, and was laid among his fathers and underwent decay; Acts 13:36

For I did not shrink from declaring to you the whole purpose of God. Acts 20:27

David, the psalmist, speaks of God having a purpose for him, and then the Apostle Paul echoes the sentiment hundreds of years later. Later, Paul also speaks of having declared the whole purpose of God to his friends. I will not presume to know what the whole purpose of God is, but I am sure it is being revealed, day to day, as we follow the Lord Jesus. Our joy is found in the pursuit and eventual fulfillment of His purposes.

Jesus' purpose:

"Now My soul has become troubled; and what shall I say, 'Father, save Me from this hour'? But for this purpose I came to this hour." John 12:27

Little children, make sure no one deceives you; the one who practices righteousness is righteous, just as He is righteous; the one who practices sin is of the devil; for the devil has sinned from the beginning. The Son of God appeared for this purpose, to destroy the works of the devil. 1 John 3:7-8

Jesus speaks more overtly of His purpose as He prays in Gethsemane. Decades later, the Apostle John, speaks of Jesus' purpose in the strongest of terms. Thankfully, we are the beneficiaries of the Lord's fulfillment of His life purpose.

Paul's purpose and ours:

We proclaim Him, admonishing every man and teaching every man with all wisdom, so that we may present every man complete in Christ. For this purpose also I labor, striving according to His power, which mightily works within me. Colossians 1:28-29

The Apostle again speaks about purpose, this time his own. He writes most clearly and directly about the subject, object, and manner of the fulfillment of that purpose. It's about Jesus. It's directed toward others. It's fulfilled by admonishing, teaching with wisdom, to present individual persons complete in Christ, according to the power of God. That's a remarkable sense of purpose.

We may similarly find ourselves engaged in that same purpose. If we are actively engaged in serving sporting people with the aim of presenting them complete in Christ, admonishing and teaching with wisdom, laboring and striving as empowered by the mighty power of God, we are. You and I share in the same purpose of God's calling as the Apostle Paul, the Apostle John, and all the saints before and behind us.

"We are His workmanship, created in Christ Jesus for good works, which He prepared beforehand that we should walk in them." Ephesians 2:10

Walk on and fulfill the Lord's purposes for your life.

Love Extravagantly
and Serve Selflessly

For many years I have been describing the primary tasks of sports chaplaincy as the following: Love extravagantly and to serve selflessly. Those are rather broad and sweeping terms and may be too vague for some to gather and to translate into action. The following paragraphs are my attempt at providing examples of each. I hope the examples inspire and possibly even provoke you to strong, extravagant, selfless love and service.

When a sports chaplain pursues redemptive relationships with coaches and competitors who are not yet Christians and may not value his or her presence, that is extravagant love.

When a character coach relentlessly attends practices, training sessions, team meetings, and any other team function in the most inconvenient hours of the day, that is extravagant love.

When a sports chaplain refuses to give up on the player he or she is mentoring, even when the competitor is more than ready to quit, to withdraw from sport, and even despairs of life itself, that is extravagant love.

When a sports chaplain actively seeks opportunities to take on the most menial tasks, to assist coaches and players with the most unpleasant chores, to find ways to be an ally to the support staff in their roles, that is selfless service.

When a character coach contemplates the genuine needs of his or her team and sees opportunities to take action, that is selfless service.

When a sports chaplain is so well connected with those he or she serves that serving them is a natural outgrowth of their love and respect and there is no thought of personal benefit, that is selfless service.

Extravagant love is, by nature, not safe, not convenient, not easy, not measured, not calculating, but is powerful, transformational, and of lasting effect.

Selfless service is, by nature, not self-centered, not normal, not common, not easy, not always fun, not always noticed or respected, but it is always appropriate, effective, and Christ-honoring.

Let's be the ones who love extravagantly and serve selflessly. By doing so we will make a powerful impact upon the world of sport and all those who live in it.

The Significance of Sports Chaplains in the 21st Century

Ministry in Sport has changed greatly in the last sixty years. It began with iconic figures and very few details about their lives. The Fellowship of Christian Athletes (FCA) was founded on this dynamic. FCA's founder, Don McClanen, selected high profile, Christian athletes to proclaim their faith in public, just as they were being used by companies to promote their products. Ministry in Sport grew through the influence of two-dimensional, heroic Christian athletes who were used by various ministries to achieve growth and financial development. FCA grew through this dynamic. The last twenty years have revealed a huge tear in the fabric of many sports ministries. Our intentions have been questioned, our integrity has been examined and our methods have been scrutinized. FCA is part and parcel of this dynamic.

The present world of sport and much of sports ministry is characterized by three primary weaknesses:

1) The prevalence of compartmentalized lives; that is a lack of integrity. This is easily seen in situations like the fall of coaches, players, and even prominent Christian athletes.

2) The horrible lie of performance-based identity. A player's sense of personal worth may rise or fall based upon his most recent performance on the field of competition. A coach's sense of God's pleasure with her may ride on her team's win/loss record. Even worse, a sport chaplain's sense of his or her being in God's will can be shaped by the relative success or failure of the teams being served. Each and all of

these scenarios are emblematic of the terrible lie that assaults the hearts of sports people.

3) The collapse of the American family structure. Most of the young men and women whom we serve are now from single parent families. They start their lives relationally and spiritually handcuffed. Worse still, if they are so blessed as to be athletically gifted, they may find that their coaches, teammates, agents, peers, lovers, even their parents and sport chaplains use the player for their own personal gain.

Sport Chaplains and Character Coaches in the 21st century are uniquely qualified to address these issues. If we will lovingly lead and serve with integrity of heart and not simply follow the culture's flow of compartmentalization, we can make a real difference. We can lead players, coaches and our colleagues in ministry toward lives of real integrity and don't treat it as a mere buzzword to impress our donors. The issue of performance-based identity is most poignant for these days and will only increase in importance in the future. The self-perpetuating cycle of broken people growing up in broken homes can be overcome by the life transforming power of the Gospel of Christ in the lives of sportspeople. Not for the sake of the masses who follow them, but for their own lives and families. They are worth it, regardless if anyone else is watching.

My challenge to you and to sports ministries globally is:

1) To conduct your ministry with a whole heart. To fully integrate the presence and power of Christ in all of life; sport, ministry, family, all of it.

2) Guard your hearts and those you serve from the

insidious lie of performance-based identity. Help them to
see that their lives are inextricably tied to the infinite value
of Christ Jesus as they are in Him.

3) Dynamically impact the lives of the people of sport
with the Gospel and thereby extend Christ's influence in
their families, teams, communities and the world.

Job, Career, or Calling?

In the spring of 2017, a statement made in passing by a coaching clinic's featured presenter, Dr. Jeff Duke. It was that some people who work in sport do it as a job, a way to make money. Others have sport as their career, demonstrating sustained excellence across time. Still others treat sport as a calling, having a strong sense of purpose for life. I'd like to develop those thoughts, one at a time.

We all know people for whom sport is their job, nothing more. This surely applies to the player who tolerates practice, travel and all that sport requires. We probably know coaches whose primary interest in sport is the paycheck. This even fits the administrator, vendor, equipment manager, or physio who has a job in sport like they would have a job in a bank, a restaurant, or driving a truck. They measure things like hours, money, and maybe productivity but nothing deeper than that.

It is likely we know people for whom sport is their career. They have excelled in at least one facet of sport and have found it to be more than just a job. They find it to be fulfilling and more rewarding than just their paycheck. These people tend to work longer hours with less complaint that those who just have jobs. They tend to commit more deeply to the people and to the institutions they serve. They tend to stay longer in the service of one university, high school, club, or team than others. These people measure achievement, long-term relationships, terms of service, and value continuity.

Many of us know, and more of us are, people who live in sport as a calling. We are vocational about sport. We have heard God's calling to the sporting world and to sporting people. We believe we were uniquely chosen, equipped, placed, and are sustained for life in sport. We trust God with situations and relationships that are beyond what career or job-oriented people would ever engage. We measure things like conversations, discipleship relationships, hours of investment in players, teams, coaches, and families. We think in terms of decades, and even generations.

If you have a job in sport, good. Be great at it, and it could become a career. If you have a sporting career, I hope it brings you rich fulfillment and reward. If you find your heart desiring even more, you may have a calling. If your calling is to live in sport, you are divinely ruined. Nothing else will satisfy your soul or engage your mind. One can quit a job or make a career change at almost any time. But one cannot quit his or her calling. God will protect His divine investment in your heart until it is fulfilled.

Availability

Let's consider another necessary quality for effective service as a sports chaplain or character coach: availability. To be available to the people one serves is of greatest importance. Finding a way to be at the right place at just the right time is most strategic for effective service and for depth of impact upon the lives of coaches, competitors and support staff. Let's consider a list of places, times and options for making oneself available.

Be available to sportspeople:

• In moments of distress—crisis and pain don't wear watches.

• To talk, to counsel, to discuss issues in sport and life in general.

• Emotionally—don't fear their pain, frustration and loss. Feel it with them.

• To simply relax with the coach or player. Give them a break from being constantly "on."

• At practice.

• In the training room.

• When it's convenient to them.

• When it's inconvenient to you.

• By phone.

• By text message.

• By email.

• In person.

If you will make yourself available you can expect to find an open heart, a trusting soul, and a warm smile from the people of sport whom you lovingly, humbly serve.

Unite My heart to Fear Your Name

For the last several years I have been encouraging coaches and competitors, sports ministry professionals and volunteers, to live their lives in sport in an integrated, holistic fashion, rather than a compartmentalized, dualistic manner. This is the Lord's way, and it is the best, most satisfying, fulfilling way to experience Christ's presence and pleasure in the experience of sport. One excellent scripture that speaks to this approach is below. I hope it encourages your heart toward a rich, full, and Christ-filled life in sport.

Teach me Your way, O Lord; I will walk in Your truth; Unite my heart to fear Your name. I will give thanks to You, O Lord my God, with all my heart, And will glorify Your name forever. Psalms 86:11-12

"Unite my heart"- To unite one's heart is to take the presently divided, compartmentalized, duplicitous heart, and to restore it to integrated, complete wholeness. Far too often, our sporting friends live in the pernicious dichotomy of sport vs. faith, rather than the graceful life of sport and faith.

Purpose. The aim of this uniting of heart, the restoration to integrity of heart, is to properly honor the name (the essence and nature) of God our Father. We who live in the sporting world are privileged to bring honor to our Lord by the way we compete, the way we serve each other, the way we love coaches, teammates, opponents, and the officials.

Process. Receiving the continual teaching of His way (selfless integrity) and the daily dwelling in His truth (God-breathed wisdom) are the pathways to a united heart. We must receive training in the Lord's way as we train and prepare for sport. We must also dwell in the Word of God for our minds and hearts to be informed by truth.

Results. With a united, integrated heart, we daily and forever express thankfulness and glorify God's name with wholehearted devotion. Our worship-work reveals the nature of the One we serve. Such a life is glorious to behold, and it inspires gratitude in the soul of the worshipful servant of Christ Jesus. My prayer is that our lives in sport are channels for expressions of thankfulness to God for all that we experience. I also pray that our daily training, teamwork, and competition reveal the nature of the Lord Jesus. The end result is that God is glorified, and our souls are filled with thankfulness.

Extravagant Love vs. Benign Tolerance

One of the values held in highest regard in US culture is "tolerance." We are implored from every angle, in the media and in the schools that we must tolerate everything and everyone around us. This value is extolled as the highest form of human virtue and should be applied to not only ethnic and religious differences, but to every form of behavior and even to those engaged in foolish, abusive or self-abusing lifestyles. I beg to differ.

Tolerance is simply too benign, too soft, too passive to be reflective of Christ Jesus' church. I believe He wants more from us than benign tolerance; He wants us to love people extravagantly. We who serve the men and women of sport are surrounded by many who are easy to love and others which we find at least distasteful and maybe even repulsive.

Here are some simple thoughts which contrast extravagant love and benign tolerance:

• Extravagant love takes risks for people. Benign tolerance is safe and secure as it keeps people at a distance.

• Extravagant love embraces people and their imperfections. Benign tolerance puts up with people we find distasteful or odd.

• Extravagant love is very costly as it pays the price to seek others' best. Benign tolerance is cheap and requires little of the one tolerating the others.

• Extravagant love is active and seeks out those whom we love. Benign tolerance is passive and feels relieved when those tolerated are not around.

• Extravagant love expects the best from others and hopes persistently. Benign tolerance expects little from others and simply hopes to not be disappointed.

• Extravagant love invests deeply in others. Benign tolerance invests shallowly, sharing only what is required.

• Extravagant love honors Christ as it directly reflects His nature. Benign tolerance honors no one as it is purely self-centered and self-protecting, honoring neither the tolerant nor the tolerated.

The obvious problem for all of us is that some people really annoy us. Some people's habits, lifestyles, behavior or cultural trappings may tear at the very fabric of our convictions and make our flesh scream for relief and distance from these people. Tolerance offers you a low cost, risk free solution to your dilemma. It is, however, not worthy of our Lord. Extravagant love is what our Lord modeled for us and has even empowered us to demonstrate. His grace is given to each of us in sufficient measure to love even the most repulsive people in our circles of relationships.

My challenge to you is to press through the easy, cheap, secure, low expectations of tolerance and take the risk, pay the cost, actively and deeply, even extravagantly love the people around you. Coaches, competitors, physios, equipment managers, club officials, athletic directors, support staff, the foolish, the perverse, the profane, the abusive, the rebellious, all of them. Jesus' blood was shed for each of them and His grace, in you, is sufficient to enable you to love them beyond your wildest imaginations. Let's love extravagantly and serve selflessly.

What Does Sports Chaplaincy Look, Sound, Taste, Smell, and Feel Like?

What does Sports Chaplaincy look like?

Sports Chaplaincy looks like sunny afternoons at football practices in the heat of August. It looks like quivering lips at the funeral visitation for a coach too soon taken from his team. It looks like the bright lights of a stadium on a fall evening. It looks like the dim lights of a locker room after a disappointing loss. In short, Sports Chaplaincy looks like opportunity. We see the hearts of men and women, boys and girls, in the glaring lights of sports arenas and in the shadows of injury, disappointment, and grief. Each of these moments looks like an opportunity to speak the life of Christ Jesus into their searching souls.

What does Sports Chaplaincy sound like?

Sports Chaplaincy sounds like loud sports arenas; their blaring music, shouting crowds, chanting fans, and bellowing announcers. It sounds like the banter between teammates in a locker room before practice. It sounds like the hushed voices and the beeps of a heat monitor in an emergency room. It sounds like the squeaks on a basketball floor during a scrimmage. It sounds like the crack of bats and pops of balls into gloves at batting practice. It sounds like sobs and sniffles while in the grieving line of mourners at a funeral wake. More simply said, Sports Chaplaincy sounds like peace. In each and all of these sounds, we experience the peace of Christ. Amid the chaos of game day and the flood of emotions in crisis, Christ Jesus carries us by His Spirit in unusual peace and assurance of His presence and provision. Sports Chaplaincy sounds like peace.

What does Sports Chaplaincy taste like?

Sports Chaplaincy tastes like pregame pasta. It tastes like sweat on your upper lip while standing at a midsummer batting practice. It tastes like a cup of coffee with the coach as you discuss the painful options for the career changes that are suddenly at hand. It tastes like the glorious post-game pizza, chicken, or sandwiches on the long bus ride home following an important road victory. It tastes like Gatorade on the sideline as you gulp down some Ibuprofen to ease the pain in aging joints. More than anything, it tastes like love. To be with the people the sports chaplain loves tastes like love, anywhere and anytime.

What does Sports Chaplaincy smell like?

I know what you're thinking, but hang on. Sports Chaplaincy smells like the barbecue smoke wafting into the stadium from the tailgate area outside. It smells like menthol from ointment rubbed on sore muscles in a training room. It smells like hot dogs and popcorn at a ballpark. Yes, it also smells of the pungent aroma in a sweaty men's locker room. But mostly it smells like competition. These olfactory stimulations prompt my heart to compete, my pulse to race, and my mind to pursue victory. I love these smells! They are as sacred as incense.

What does Sports Chaplaincy feel like?

Sports Chaplaincy feels like pain in one's joints. It feels like breathless exhilaration after a thrilling victory. It feels like bitter grief after a disappointing loss. It feels like the rush of pride when a player breaks through a performance barrier. It feels like death when a coach is exposed for cheating. It feels like joy when relationships are restored. It feels like discomfort when riding a bus through the night after a rainy road loss to a rival. It feels like life. All of life's kaleidoscope of emotions are distilled into the sporting experience for the competitors, the coaches, the support staff, and even the sport chaplain. Sports Chaplaincy feels like life. Isn't it wonderful?

Sports Chaplaincy, when experienced with an open heart, an inquisitive mind, with fully engaged emotions, and an active body is rich with sensory perception. Go ahead, jump in with both feet. Plunge into the depths of sports chaplaincy. See its marvels. Hear its sonic flood of music and voice. Fill your mouth with its delicious tastes. Breathe in its every aroma. Feel its joy, pain, exhilaration, and grief. It's worth the risk, and the reward will capture your soul. Our Lord walks with us through each and all these experiences. He sanctifies them with His presence and consecrates them in our hearts.

How To Start:

Orientation and Training

Where one lives in the world will largely dictate the process of orientation, training, and beginning to serve as a sports chaplain or character coach. Some regions or nations have well defined processes and entities dedicated to the identification, recruiting, orientation, training, placement, and mentoring the service of sports chaplains. Many more do not.

In the appendix of this book there are links to a number of sports ministries and sports chaplaincy entities that can provide the necessary training for anyone to serve. Please investigate those nearest you. The best way to walk through this process is in person. For many of us around the world, this is not possible due to geography, language, culture, or governmental restrictions.

For those of us in the USA, this process varies widely depending upon one's affilliation with a sports ministry or the lack thereof.

Below is a process that I have been using with my colleagues of the Fellowship of Christian Athletes in the Midwest Region. I hope it serves you well.

Orientation and Training Outline

Orientation

• 1 hour in person or on line at www.global-sportschaplaincy.org

• Majors on FCA Vision, Mission, Values, definitions, profile of Character Coach, needs of sportspeople, and opportunities to serve.

- Q and A.

Training—In person (3 hours)

1. Introductions and thank you: (10 minutes)
2. Part 1 Introduction
   a. Introduce F.C.A. (15 minutes)
           o Vision, Mission, Values
           o Strategy
           o Methods—F.C.A. Character Coaches:
           Engage, Equip, and Empower.
   b. Character Coach Overview (5 minutes)
   c. Profile of a Sportsperson (10 minutes)
   d. Key Qualities of a Character Coach (10 minutes)
   e. A Biblical Foundation for Character Coaching
   (10 minutes)
3. Part 2—Be Seen (20-30 minutes)
4. Part 3—Be Known (20-30 minutes)
5. Part 4—Be Heard (20-30 minutes)
6. A Process for Beginning to Serve as an FCA Character
   Coach (10 minutes)
7. Commissioning to Service as FCA Character Coaches
   (10 minutes)

Beginning to serve as an FCA Character Coach.

1. Connect with FCA Staff in your area to:
   a. Review and sign the FCA Character Coach Code
   of Conduct.
   b. Discuss service of designated team(s) and to
   engage with the coaching staff.

c. Develop a preseason game plan for service.

d. Communicate periodically to monitor progress, to solve problems, for encouragement, to mentor, etc.

e. Conduct a post-season review.

Your First 30 Days Serving as a Sports Chaplain

During an FCA Sports Chaplain conference in Kansas City, Missouri (USA), a number of my colleagues who are rather new to their service asked a lot of questions about the process of beginning to serve. Certainly everyone's place of service is different and the circumstances vary widely, but below is an attempt at a list of things one should do in his or her first thirty days of service. I hope it's helpful.

In your first thirty days of serving as a sports chaplain or character coach, I recommend that you:

• Thank God daily for the opportunity and privilege you have.

• Thank the coaches and/or ministry staff that opened the door to you.

• Get an appointment with the head coach to discuss details for your service (preferences, timing, things to be sure to do, things to be sure to avoid).

• Attend practices, speaking to everyone who gives you eye contact. Introduce yourself, but don't use a title to describe your role. It will get around.

• Memorize the team roster by name, uniform number, position, and home town. All are important.

• Arrange to meet personally with anyone to responds to your initial contacts to build relationships and to seek ways to serve them.

• If on a college campus, meet the NCAA compliance officer, introduce yourself, ask how he/she would like you to communicate about opportunities with and for student-athletes. Make this person an ally, not an enemy.

• Pray for the coaches, competitors, and support staff you are serving.

• Learn to see the faces, to hear the voices, and to feel the experiences of those you serve in your devotional reading, in your moments of contemplation and prayer, and as you travel to and from sporting venues.

• Journal your interactions with those you serve from preseason through postseason. Save the journals for reading in annual preparation prior to new seasons.

• Set your heart to serve at all times.

• Set your heart to love in all circumstances.

• Prepare to stride joyfully into the next thirty days.

As a New Season Approaches

For many of us, especially my friends and colleagues in the USA, a new season of sport is about to begin. The start of a new school year brings with it a new fall sports schedule and the preseason practices that precede it. I would like to recommend some simple matters that may help you be fully prepared as a new season approaches.

Memorize the team roster and pray for each one. Ask the coach or an office person for the team roster, take the time and effort to memorize the names and numbers. Match those with their faces, and you're on the way to building relationships.

Meet with the head coach to discuss his or her points of emphasis for your work together. Ask about specific ways you can serve the coaches and the players. Ask for some boundaries for when and where it is most appropriate for you to be present, and maybe when and where your presence is not appropriate. It's better to discover these ahead of time than through the discomfort of embarrassment or confrontation. Ask the coach how you may pray for him/her, the staff, and the players.

Attend as many preseason practices as you can. You can observe the coaches and how they coach. You can observe the players and perceive many things about their attitudes, approach to work, the team's cohesion, etc. This is also the best place to work on roster memorization as you can see numbers, faces, and match them to the players' names. This is also the perfect environment for prayers of intercession as you think about each player and coach. Pray for them and for

God's purposes to be accomplished in each one.

Above all, use the preseason to build relationships. Greet everyone you can and see who responds well. Pursue those warmest responses first, ask good questions, serve, and communicate loving respect.

To occupy yourself with these four activities, especially in the preseason weeks, is of greatest importance. Invest some time, some inconvenience, and some sweat in wise preparation. It will pay off richly in the ensuing weeks and months.

Building Relationships with Coaches

As we serve the men and women, boys and girls in sport, there is a set of people with whom it is most strategic to build relationships, trust, and confidence. They are called, "coaches." To earn the trust and respect of sports coaches is neither easy nor quick, but it is vital to serving them and all whom they coach well.

I learned early on in my service of sports teams that having the trust of the coaching staff and each coach on it, is most important. Think about it this way, if the coach trusts me, he or she will call me about an issue with a competitor. If the coach distrusts me, he or she will tell the competitors, "Stay away from that guy," or even worse. Further, when I earn the coach's trust, suddenly his heart is within reach, her family can be loved and served, and in fact everyone in the coach's sphere of influence is suddenly in range of our ministry.

Below is a list of very practical and proven methods for building relationships with coaches:

· Meet them where they are—that is usually at practice and in their offices.

· Learn the best time to speak with them, face to face. That may be prior to practice starting. It may be before or after team meetings. Experiment and learn.

· Take an interest in their families. Ask about spouses, children, their interests away from sport, etc.

· Ask questions about their coaching pilgrimage, their background in the sport, and look for points of connection with other coaches in your network.

· Ask about what gives them satisfaction, a sense of satisfaction, in their coaching.

· Ask them how you may be of service to the coach and his or her families.

· If the coach asks about finding a church in the community, share several good options, not just your own. Ask questions like, "For what kind of a church are you looking?"

· Take note of everything in his or her office. Coaches usually have items displayed which reveal what they love and respect. Notice the books on the shelves, the photos on the desk or on the wall, balls, medals, rings, certificates, ribbons, etc. that speak to their accomplishments. Choose one item and ask a question about it. Stories will follow.

· If you dare, ask this question. "Why do you coach?" Stop and listen. You may gain more insight from this question than anything else you could do.

The bottom line in all of these methods and all the relationship building is simple. For the coach to know and to trust you is the pathway to his or her heart. They are generally overwhelmed with responsibilities, they have little to no job security, they have thousands of critics, but they have almost no one who will consistently encourage, love, and support them. We get to be those trusted encouragers, if we don't act like sports fans.

One sign that you are doing well and building relationships of trust, with coaches is if when greeting you the coach says, "Hi Coach." For the coach to bestow the sport's most sacred title upon you is an immediate sign that you are welcomed into their world with honor. If coaches speak of you as being, "a part of our staff," or "an important part of the program," you are crushing it. Please take my challenge and develop relationships with coaches as a matter of highest priority, and you will find it to bear fruit that will remain.

Building Relationships with Support Staff

Last week we discussed the development of relationships with coaches. Today I'd like to have us think about how to develop relationships with a sporting team's support staff. This includes a wide variety of people who support the coaches and competitors on a team.

The people I have in mind include:
- Athletic administrators
- Athletic trainers (physios)
- Equipment managers
- Operations managers
- Office personnel
- Team doctors

One may wonder why building relationships with these people is important. I would simply say that they are as valuable to God as is the most productive or highest profile player, the head coach, or anyone else associated with the team. In addition, building relationships with these people can make your service of the team easier, more effective, and deeper than it could ever be without their insight, expertise, and partnership.

Having a relationship of trust with the athletic trainer or physiotherapist, can be of tremendous value as he or she can inform you of injuries, upcoming surgeries, and other situations encountered by players. This information often leads to ministry opportunities for me.

Having favor with the athletic administration could be the determining factor as to a sports chaplain's access to secure areas; practice, sidelines, locker rooms, etc.; as well as travel with a team. Without that relationship, the character coach is an easy one to drop from the passenger list.

The equipment managers of our teams have become friends, allies, and trusted sources of administration for me. I can quickly learn many details about practice schedules, travel plans, and more from the numerous managers around a college football practice.

To know and offer to serve the operations manager for a team is a wise and effective relationship to build. These people have to manage most of the logistics for a team's travel and the whole process of game day. They are usually quite stressed, and when we have an encouraging voice, hands ready to serve, and express thankfulness for their work, we build relationship quickly.

The head coach's secretary, the office manager, and other personnel around the coaches' offices are the gatekeepers to the staff's inner sanctum. Make the office manager your friend. I was privileged to be married to one of these and her influence with four different coaching staffs and the daily lives of 100+ student-athletes each year could not be overstated.

Finally, to be familiar, even just acquainted, with the team doctors can be of tremendous value to you and to those you serve. The doctor can allow you into the personal life of injured competitors, can give you access to family and to moments of crisis for the player (surgery center, emergency room, etc.) so that you may serve most effectively.

In summary, a sports team's support staff can be of

immeasurable value to your efforts to serve the coaching staff and competitors on the team. Let's be sure to love and serve the support staff in a similar way as to how we love and serve the competitors. Their eternal souls are of infinite worth, and they are within our sphere of influence and responsibility.

Beginnings and Endings
of Sports Seasons

No matter the sport with which you serve, there is a natural rhythm to the season. Each season has a beginning and an end. Most have a pre-season and a post-season. We would be wise to understand these natural rhythms and to shape our work so as to take advantage of both the beginning and the end of the season. Following are some thoughts about both the beginning and ending of sports seasons.

Beginning of a season—The great thing about this part of the season is that everyone starts undefeated. Hope beats strongly in the hearts of every team and each player and coach during this part of the season. As soon as the first competition is completed, half of all the teams competing now have losses. Let the hope and anticipation of the new season work for you as you speak with everyone in terms filled with hope, expectation, excitement, and anticipation of good things.

The downside of this part of the season is that some have expectations that range from unrealistic to laughable. If we are wise we will help these, less than reasonable, players or coaches to focus on the daily process of preparation and competition, over against a set of results that they hope validate their optimism. Talk in terms of embracing the process of development and becoming the team they hope to be at the end of the season. You may see their disappointment coming before they do.

When speaking with team leaders (coaches, club managers, etc.), set the boundaries for your service and the expectations for when, where, and how you will serve the team. Seek to establish this and to maintain a consistency of service without regard to the ups and downs that accompany most seasons of sport.

End of a season—The great part about this part of the season is that we now know what kind of team we have. The process and the results have revealed the nature of our team. Some teams compete like champions and enjoy the rewards of such performance. Others finish well below the .500 line and lick their wounds as the season mercifully ends. Still others find themselves mired in the mediocrity of the middle of the standings. In any case, there is a finality to the end of any season.

Be mindful that for some or many, the end of this season is also the end of their careers. At every level of sport, the end of sports seasons bring the end of careers. When you are aware of such, speak clearly and affirm those who exit the sport. A simple thank you card, a well-crafted letter, a chat over coffee, or a visit to your home for dinner are all powerful ways to express your heart and God's heart to those who finish their sporting careers.

Consider those who may be terminated at season's end. The sports world can be cold and cruel to those who underperform or seem to be a "poor fit." It is of immense value to those who leave the team that you show faithfulness and loyalty when they are terminated. Pursue them with calls, text messages, tweets, however you can; find a way to express your support, to assure them of your prayers, and to communicate your respect. Most of their colleagues and friends don't know what to say or how to respond. We need the emotional intelligence and grace to love those who find themselves adrift and seeking new employment.

Finally, after the season it is always wise to meet with the team leaders (coaches, club managers, etc.) to evaluate, to review, and to discuss your service of the team. Seek their ideas, adjustments, and vision for the season to come.

Let the natural rhythms of the sporting season work in your favor. Take advantage of their virtues and beware of their vices. Use these seasonal advantages to enable you to love the people of sport in your charge extravagantly and to serve them selflessly.

How to Serve People:
Teams

"I love college football!"

In December of 2019 I delivered a talk to the football teams of Greenville University and Olivet Nazarene University at the banquet for the NCCAA Victory Bowl. The game was to be played the next day, November 23 in Greenville, Illinois.

An outline of my talk is below. I hope the ideas therein challenge your thoughts about sport and its value to Christians in sport.

Introduction: Think about what you love about college football.

· For 26 seasons now I have been our team's chaplain and get-back coach.

· Untold hundreds of man-hours of preparation by dozens of people, across six days of each week's practice, training, video review, teaching, and scheming; all compressed into one-hundred-fifty to one-hundred-eighty six second explosions of fury and orchestrated chaos.

· Each step, each glance, each hesitation, each moment of insight, each explosive movement has immense weight and importance for the success or failure of any given play.

· The teamwork, comradery, selflessness, attention to detail, and tolerance of discomfort needed to excel in this sport are uncommon traits in our society.

· And, it's fun!

· I love college football for another, far superior reason as well. It is an environment and an endeavor in which we may experience the presence and pleasure of the Lord Jesus as an act of worship.

Text—Romans 12:1-2 This text contains big ideas.

"Therefore I urge you, brethren, by the mercies of God, to present your bodies a living and holy sacrifice, acceptable to God, which is your spiritual service of worship. And do not be conformed to this world, but be transformed by the renewing of your mind, so that you may prove what the will of God is, that which is good and acceptable and perfect."

1. I urge you, brothers, by the mercies of God.

    a. This is not a suggestion.

    b. Not a wish.

    c. Not a hope.

    d. He urges, he exhorts, and he beseeches his brothers.

    e. By the mercies of God. The ground upon which we consider his next thoughts are the mercies of God.

    f. By the mercies of God, he urges his brothers.

2. Present your bodies, a living and holy sacrifice, acceptable to God, which is your spiritual service of worship.

    a. The presentation of your bodies is a:

A living sacrifice, not a dead one. It is a daily, hourly, play by play, practice by practice sacrifice.

A holy sacrifice, set apart for God. Football is not played behind God's back. It's set apart for Him.

An acceptable sacrifice, not something tolerated by God, rather it's an acceptable, well-pleasing sacrifice. You can expect to experience God's pleasure as you present your body as a sacrifice through sport.

This is your spiritual service of worship. Beyond an activity that God would tolerate until you can get to worship at church. Football itself is an environment for and an activity in which we worship the Lord Jesus.

b. When you step onto the field to train, to practice, or to compete in football, you have the privilege of presenting your body as a living and holy sacrifice, acceptable to God, which is your spiritual service of worship.

3. Do not be conformed to this world.

a. The world would have you separate who you are as a Christ-following man from who you are as a football player.

b. You, the excellent student, the loving son, the loyal brother, the faithful friend, vs. you, the raging, almost out of control, barbaric, maniacal football player. Which is the real you?

c. Greek thinking, prevailing cultural dualism would have you experience life as two separate people.

d. Hebrew thinking, God-honoring integrity would have you be the same man, all the time, regardless of environment or circumstance.

e. Do not be conformed to this world.

4. Rather, be transformed by the renewing of your mind, so that you may prove what the will of God is, that which is good and acceptable and perfect.

a. Transform the way you think about football, about competition.

b. To compete is to strive together. Together, not against.

c. If we have no opponent for competition, we only have practice. If we don't turn on the score board, we just have another practice.

d. To compete is to test each other as we both strive to be our best, to grow, to develop, and ultimately to become all God has purposed for us to be.

e. As we compete we prove or test what the will of God is, and we find it to be:

Good—we find the will of God to be good for us.

Acceptable—we find the will of God to be well-pleasing to us.

Perfect—we find the will of God to be perfect or complete.

5. Football players, coaches, support staff, may I challenge you with the Apostle Paul's words?

a. I urge you, brothers, by the mercies of God.

b. Present your bodies a living and holy sacrifice, acceptable to God, which is your spiritual service of worship.

c. Do not be conformed to this world, but.

d. Be transformed by the renewing of your mind, so that you may prove what the will of God is, that which is good and acceptable and perfect.

I love college football because it is an environment and an endeavor in which we may experience the presence and the pleasure of the Lord Jesus as an act of worship.

I pray you also experience our Lord's presence and His pleasure each time you prepare, train, practice, and compete.

Ministry in Preseason Baseball

Each spring in Southern Illinois arrives with soaking rain, blooming flowers, greening grass, and baseball. For the last several springs, the blossoms of April have brought me a new season of opportunity to serve the players, coaches, support staff, and management of the Southern Illinois Miners of the Frontier League of professional baseball. This is a rare privilege.

The Miners arrive in Marion, Illinois in late April having been signed during the winter, returning from last season's team, or having been recruited during the recent combine for independent teams. They arrive with hearts full of promise, bodies full of talent, minds full of questions, and souls full of anxiety. We tend to get players either on their way up or on their way down in baseball. Some have completed their college baseball careers but were not selected in the draft by a team affiliated with a major league team. They still believe they can play and hope playing in this league will give them the chance to play their way onto an affiliated team's roster. Some come to us after years of playing with affiliated team of minor league baseball. For any number of reasons, they have been released and have found their way to Southern Illinois. They intend to retool one part of their game and to return to their climb toward the big leagues. Others have been released from minor league clubs and simply don't want to get a regular job and be grownups. In any case, they are desperate to play baseball, or they would not be here.

All these factors leave their hearts in a rather vulnerable

place. At a glance one would not perceive this but understanding their station in baseball makes it readily apparent.
Like most gifted athletes, these young men have the poise,
swagger, bravado, and air of confidence that some find off
putting. They wear these traits like body armor, guarding
their hearts from the doubts and insecurities that stalk their
preseason workouts and the sleepless nights of late April and
early May.

My role of service in this situation is simple but has many
facets. I aim to serve, each and all, as they are with the club.
Whether they are here for a week, a season, or for years, I
seek their best interests and the Lord's purposes in their
lives. This level of baseball affords me a unique opportunity
and an immense responsibility. These young men are not
burdened with enormous salaries or plush amenities that
harden hearts and inflate egos. Their hearts are much closer
to the surface and are quicker to hear the words of an older
man who cares for them and wants the best for them, with
no strings attached.

Here's what that looks like on a typical day of the
preseason:

• I download and print out the team roster so that I can
memorize names, uniform numbers, and faces of each player
and coach.

• I drive the 16 miles to the ballpark anticipating
conversations, remembering relationships from past
seasons, and preparing my heart in prayer.

• I arrive at the ballpark, pass through the player's
entrance, walk by the clubhouse, and exit to the hitting cage.

- At some point in the preseason, Mike Pinto, the COO and field manager of the club, invites me to introduce myself and my role with the team. For this I am very grateful.

- I will come to as many workouts as possible, and on game days I'll arrive in time for batting practice.

- I will greet players at the hitting cage, group by group as they hit, or I'll join them on the field as they stretch, throw, and take batting practice.

- I make it a point to meet each player, to ask about his hometown, and about his path to this place in baseball. To hear their stories helps us to connect and for me to understand more of who they are. I also get a sense of how they perceive this point along their journey through professional baseball.

- Once introduced, some players will seek me out and others will begin to avoid me. I am, however, hard to avoid. I just keep showing up.

- During the preseason I will identify a player to be the player representative for Baseball Chapel. He will be the one I rely on to inform his teammates of Bible study and game day chapel times and locations during the season. He is also the player who helps gather players for chapels held on the road, led by the home team's chapel leader.

- During these days of preseason, we will discuss the process for Sunday home game Baseball Chapels and the best day and time for a Bible study during each home stand.

- Occasionally I will have the opportunity to meet with a player or coach individually, over breakfast or coffee.

- Occasionally I will have the privilege to walk with a player or a coach through a crisis. We have walked with players as they lost family members, with support staff through cancer treatments, through relationship difficulties, injuries, surgeries, death, and other matters confidentiality forbids me to discuss.

• As preseason progresses, the roster is trimmed down until the opening day team is selected. That means many players will be traded or released, thus ending their stay in Marion. This is always painful and always strains relationships. Hearts once full of hope and expectation are suddenly crushed by feelings of rejection, failure, and even despair. For some, this is the end of their lives in baseball. For others, they will seek new opportunities elsewhere. In any case, I feel the grief of relationships lost.

Many people have said that professional baseball is a great game, but a terrible business. I have a sense of that each preseason. We start with a large group of hopeful, excited young men, and day by day a couple are released, a few are traded, some new ones arrive, and by opening day, the business is complete. Suddenly the roster is set, the games begin, and everything seems bright, new, and exciting.

Baseball, like spring in Southern Illinois, is full of new life, thunderstorms, sunshine, fear, joy, fulfillment, disappointment, runs, hits, errors, wins, and losses. This is why I'm here, to walk along with the players, coaches, management, and support staff through all of it. To do so is one of my life's greatest joys.

College Football Calendar
of Ministry Opportunities

During a conversation with a colleague who is serving a Division I college football program (American Football), he remarked that some of the important dates, seasons, and opportunities associated with college football were a complete mystery to him. After many seasons, I have taken for granted much of that information and the ministry opportunities associated with them.

Below, please take a few moments to consider which of these seasonal opportunities may be yours as well as mine. These are from my perspective as a Division I FCS program and could be moderately different if you are at a Division I FBS school, Division II, Division III, or an NAIA school. I hope these thoughts raise some new opportunities to serve for you.

January –

• This is a pressure packed month for recruiting as coaches are both in players' homes and welcoming them and their families to campus.

• During the week of the Division I national championship, the American Football Coaches Association hosts their annual convention. This is an excellent place to connect with coaches from all across the USA and even abroad. http://www.afca.com/article/article.php?id=Convention_News

• There are also some Glazier Clinics held during January, also a great place to interact with coaches. For dates and locations of clinics, see http://www.glazierclinics.com/coaching_clinics/cities_and_dates

February –

• The NCAA letter of intent signing date is always the first Wednesday of February. This is even better than Christmas Day for coaches as they see years of recruiting come to fruition as their fax machines buzz with completed forms.

• This month and the weeks prior to spring football practices make for a good time to meet with coaches, to plan for the spring, summer, and even fall.

• These weeks can also be a good time to interject a weekly discussion on leadership or a Bible study. If you offer it, this may be the perfect time to start such a ministry with the coaching staff.

• This period may also be a good time to meet with the aspiring team leaders to help them prepare for their roles of leadership.

March –

• At some point, Division I and II have spring football practices. Division I gets 15 practices, and I believe Division II gets a few less.

• To be at these practices, even for just a few minutes, pays huge dividends. Everyone knows there are no games on spring Saturdays. When they see you at practice, they know it's neither glamorous nor convenient, but it speaks to your commitment to them.

April and May -

• Most teams will have a spring game of some sort. It may be similar to a real game with the team broken into two halves, or it could be a scripted scrimmage with lots of prescribed down and distance, game situations, and engineered stressful moments laid out ahead of time.

• April and early May is also a time when coaches can go on the road to observe high school junior players in the recruiting process. Rules severely limit the contact they can have, but this is often when players are given invitations to summer camps on the school's campus so the coaches can get first-hand information, reliable times and measurements, and a look into the player's personality.

• Being available to simply drop in on coaches and to ask them about family, travel, their summer plans, or the players' academic performance is a solid way to build relationship in this season.

June and July –

• This is summer camp season, and most teams will host numerous camps. Camps provide a great environment for ministry, mostly as we show up, serve, and build relationships with the coaches hosting the events as well as the coaches attending with their players.

• Individual camps—these are for assessment of players in their recruiting process.

• Team camps—these vary from state to state but usually allow whole teams to compete in full pads.

• Elite camps—these will usually focus on a particular position group and are usually by invitation only.

• 7 on 7 tournaments—these are focused on the passing game of football and usually run one day.

August –

• This is GO TIME! Months of planning and preparation

have gone into the preseason process and coaches work well over 16 hours a day during this season between early August and the start of school.

• The preseason is a wonderful environment for ministry as the players are sequestered from normal life, they spend all day and all evening together, and if you are allowed to be at practices, team meetings, or team meals, get there! Being with them in these days, even without anything programmatic happening, builds your bond with them like nothing else.

• Over the years I have done many Sunday morning, 6:00 chapel talks on the 50-yard line prior to a team stretch. I have done team building exercises with our teams for nearly 15 years. I have eaten countless team breakfasts, lunches, and dinners with players and coaches.

• Once school starts, things find a more normal rhythm, and the NCAA twenty-hour rule takes effect. The coaches are limited as to the time they can spend with the players. This also gives us opportunity as we are not limited by the rule, and we can enhance the coaches' roles by leading, encouraging, serving, and loving the players.

September through November –

• This is the regular season of college football. Its weekly schedule is similar to this (some will vary slightly):

• Sunday is usually an off day for the players or the coaches may have them come in to lift weights and stretch as well as watch video of the last game. The coaches grind on this day, reviewing video of the last game, grading player performances, watching video of the next opponent, and more.

- Monday is either an off day or a return to practice. The coaches are usually now working on the game plan for the next opponent on Saturday. Monday practices are often a return to fundamentals and skill enhancement drills.

- Tuesday is normally the day to install particular elements of the upcoming game plan. They will drill these until they are in sync. There is also a lot of video review to be done by the players with their coaches.

- Wednesday and Thursday are for practice and preparation of this week's points of emphasis.

- Friday is either a walk through (at home), or travel to the site of Saturday's game, or both. Many teams hold their team chapel on Friday nights in the team hotel, before or after the team dinner.

- Saturday—game day. The timing varies widely, depending upon time for the kickoff, but some teams will hold their team chapel prior to or following the team's pregame meal. Some teams will hold a Protestant chapel on Friday night and a Roman Catholic mass on Saturday. This day is full of ministry opportunity simply because of the pressure it contains and the significance of each play. Everyone feels the urgency and the pressure to succeed, including the chaplain.

- Many programs will hold a team banquet where they will wrap up the season, give team awards, and say goodbye to the senior players. This affords one opportunities to serve at the banquet, to say goodbye to senior players, and otherwise to wrap up the season.

Late November through December –

• This begins the post-season part of the year.

o That could mean a bowl game. If Division I FBS teams win six games, they are bowl eligible and could be chosen for a bowl game. If so, that means more practices, and that's what the coaches value. It means another game; that's what the players value. It could mean a warm weather destination; that's what the fans value. It usually means a good amount of cash; that's what the school administrators value.

o If in Division I FCS, Division II, Division III, or NAIA, the post-season could mean a playoff bid. These divisions play a tournament to determine a national champion. This simply extends the opportunities for the chaplain by 1, 2, 3, or even 4 weeks.

• This is also often the most painful part of the year as coaches are fired, leave of their own volition for other opportunities, and uproot their families for their next coaching spot. Relationships are broken, feelings are bruised, loyalty is challenged, and many other relational issues bring opportunity to our door. We must possess tremendous emotional intelligence to navigate these stormy waters wisely and well.

• These months also intensify the recruiting process as coaches will be on the road making home visits, scheduling campus visits, and otherwise connecting with players for their programs' future. Thankfully, NCAA rules require that they stop recruiting for some holiday time with family. Otherwise some would surely be making calls to players on Christmas morning.

There it is, a thumbnail sketch of a college football calendar with some notes for ministry opportunities. Please take time to study your program's schedule, feel its pulse, smell its culture, and live in its rhythm. Your heart will awaken you to the opportunities to serve as you hear the Savior whisper in your ear, "This is the way. Walk in it."

Ministry in Minor League Baseball

The first weeks of May bring with them the beginning of the Frontier League Baseball season. The players reported to Rent One Park in Marion, Illinois on April 29 for the 2015 season of the Southern Illinois Miners. The Frontier League is a set of teams in independent professional baseball. Their being independent simply means these teams are not affiliated with a major league organization. The salaries are small, but the hearts are large and passionate.

I am thrilled to be serving this particular club because of the culture being nurtured by the manager, Mike Pinto. Mike has been the manager of the Miners since their first season in 2006, having declined opportunities to join other clubs of independent baseball as well as affiliated teams. Mike brings a professionalism and an attention to detail that is uncommon at this level of baseball.

Among the factors that make for good ministry with this club and at this level of professional baseball are these:

My relationship with the manager and the coaches. From the first day of my service, Mike has welcomed me into every part of the team's life. I am careful to not overstep my bounds, but when I consult him with opportunities to serve, Mike is quick to make room for our ministry efforts. In addition, being intentional to build relationships with the coaches (hitting, pitching, bench, etc.) and the support staff (clubhouse manager, athletic trainers, ushers, front office, etc.) has borne fruit as well.

Baseball is a "hang out" culture. To build relationships with baseball players, one must simply show up, hang out, and talk about whatever comes up. For type A people, like your humble correspondent, this is often difficult. I am much better with an agenda and a set of objectives, but to faithfully serve this group requires flying by the seat of one's pants. To stand around the hitting cage as batting practice takes place is invaluable. To lean on the dugout railing and to idly chat wins favor and trust. To ask questions about family, hometowns, college teammates, or one's path through baseball that landed him in Marion, Illinois is the stuff of relationship and the foundation for more meaningful and spiritual conversations in the future.

A four to one ratio of appearances to talks works best. It seems to require four appearances at batting practices to each Sunday home Baseball Chapel talk to be effective. The more faithful I am to make time to hang out at batting practice, the more the players and coaches trust me and the more they will take their pregame time to sit with me in the dugout after batting practice on Sunday afternoon to hear my five minute talk and to pray with me.

My home is sixteen miles from the ballpark. From my garage to my parking place at the baseball park is short enough for me to make time to be there. If it were 30 miles, it would be significantly more difficult but would still be worth it. If it were 50 miles, I would likely not serve well.

These players are desperate to play baseball. If I told you the amount some of these young men are paid you wouldn't believe it. They live with host families who provide a room, meals, and laundry when the players are in town. Some of our players have recently exhausted their college baseball eligibility and were not taken by the major league draft. Some of our players have already played a number of years in affiliated baseball but have been released by those clubs.

Some of them have been in other independent baseball organizations and still others have simply been out of baseball for a while due to injury. Some of them are Latino players from the Dominican Republic, Venezuela, Panama, or Mexico and staying in baseball allows them to stay in the USA and to send some money home to family. All of them are twenty-seven years or younger. All of these factors lead to a desperation to be in baseball that enables them to press through low pay and often rather poor conditions. This desperation also places their hearts right at the surface. After earning their trust, I find them eager to ask for advice, to air problems, or to ask for prayer. They come to Baseball Chapel services on Sundays and excitedly make time for our discussions of scripture midweek during home stands.

Baseball Chapel's legacy and reputation in baseball is strong. This ministry has long been the standard for faithful ministry within professional baseball at every level. It is of tremendous value for me to be able to open a chapel talk by saying, "This afternoon, at every level of baseball from Yankee Stadium in New York to stadiums in the Dominican Republic to Rent One Park in Marion, Illinois, men just like you are sitting in dugouts to pray and to hear the truth of scripture applied to their lives in baseball." Baseball Chapel provides handouts, in English and in Spanish, that we can download from their website to use with the players, coaches, umpires, management, wives of players, and even support staff. The faithfulness of Baseball Chapel and that of their wide network of men who serve in their ministry have paved the way for many relative newcomers, like me.

If you should have opportunity to serve a minor league baseball club, if you have any background in the sport, if you are adept at "hanging out," or even if you can make yourself do it, please consider serving in this way. Please consider the various factors listed above as potential keys to effective ministry and jump in with both feet. I have just begun season nine with our club and cannot wait to see what will occur this summer.

Between the middle of May and the early weeks of September there are a myriad of opportunities for the Lord Jesus to invade the lives of desperate young men, grizzled older coaches, ambitious management personnel, and the families of each and all.

Sports Chaplain Principles and Best Practices for Serving Professional Sportspeople

Walt Enoch—as told to Roger Lipe November, 2009

Walt Enoch began serving professional athletes in 1970 when only the Los Angeles Dodgers and Chicago Cubs had chapel leaders. He was already serving the St. Louis Cardinals when Baseball Chapel began its ministry. Walt also served the St. Louis Football Cardinals before their move to Arizona and has served the St. Louis Rams since they arrived in town. For two years he had a ministry with the NHL's St. Louis Blues. For many years he worked to oversee all of the baseball chapel leaders in the Cardinals minor league cities.

Walt believes, "FCA (Fellowship of Christian Athletes) should be the vehicle for serving the people of professional sports." Walt describes the role of the sport chaplain in this way, "to bring Christ to the players, coaches and support staff in their life situation and to serve them however you can."

Among Walt's core values for serving in this role are:
• Love
• Service
• Acceptance of others (teach it to them)
• Christ-centered ministry

Walt's points of emphasis for effectively serving professional sportspeople will be listed under the following categories:

- Relationships
- Attitude
- Presence
- Strategies, Methods and Resources

Relationships –

- In NFL Football—the chaplain serves at the pleasure of the head coach. That relationship is most important. Walt says, "He runs the machine. I'm just a spark plug."

- Walt opens these relationships with a letter of welcome to the head coach, by arranging to meet with him and by offering to serve. The head coach then tells him what he wants the chaplain to do.

- He makes it a point to introduce and offer service to all in the organization, trainers, doctors, office personnel, etc.

- With NFL players, Walt recognizes that the pro football player comes from a college atmosphere where he is considered highly. Don't be put off by it but understand who they are.

- In Major League Baseball—Baseball Chapel appoints the chapel leaders and works through an application and interview process.

- The Baseball Chapel leader mostly relates to the players. Seldom do coaches, managers or support personnel participate in chapels.

- With MLB players, Walt recognizes that these players come up through the minor league system with very little money and a tough road to reach the major leagues.

- One should not expect a strong sense of community among professional sports teammates off the field of competition. Once out of the locker room, it's seldom that they spend a lot of time with their teammates.

• As one is building his relationship with players, it's important to not be seen as a part of the club's organization. If one is too closely tied to the management, it could compromise his trust among the players.

• I asked Walt about how to handle transitions for players and coaches (trades, free agency, waivers, firings, etc...) and he said that if your relationship is strong, call the player or coach. Arrange to meet with the player or coach. Encourage, counsel, console and work to maintain the relationship if at all possible. Though it's difficult, some relationships have been able to last for many years beyond the player's career in sport.

• Walt made a point to not forget the players when their playing careers are over. He arranges a separate Bible study for former players. (It's best not to mix current and former players. It's awkward for both sets of people.)

• With professional sportspeople, serving their spouses and children is an important part of effective ministry. Many times it's the most mundane tasks which win the chaplain favor and trust with the family and consequently, the player or coach.

These may include:

    o Driving family members to the airport to drop off or pick someone up.

    o Helping families move into their new home or to move out when traded, fired or waived.

    o Helping families find real estate agents, schools,

day care, family doctors, churches, etc...

• Walt and his wife have found that holidays (Easter, Thanksgiving, Christmas and others) were outstanding opportunities to serve players' and coaches' families through hospitality. Having them in their home made a real impact with the players and their families.

• We discussed the high-profile nature of many players and how to deal with those who fail publically, especially moral failure. How should the chaplain handle those situations?

    o Love them.

    o Seek them out.

    o Don't confront their behavior, but rather be available to them, and when they open the subject, be clear, loving and direct.

Attitude –

• I asked Walt about some necessary character traits and attitudes for a sports chaplain to develop, and he listed these:

    o A servant's heart

    o No favoritism (treat everyone the same)

    o A reliance upon Scripture

    o Be invisible to outsiders.

    o Know your place and stay in it.

    o See yourself as a guest of the club.

    o Be mindful of who you are working for, (God), and serve Him.

• I asked about some attitudes to avoid:

    o Don't ever think of "using" players, only serving them.

o Don't use the players for personal gain, rather than serving them.

o Don't use one's relationship with the team to raise his profile.

o Don't be too forward in approaching players.

o Do not act like a fan.

o Don't ask them for contributions. Ever.

o Don't become involved in their finances.

o Don't refer financial services to the players unless the player asks you for your opinion. Don't serve as the agent for a financial manager, especially one who approaches you.

o Don't get entangled in dealing with sports memorabilia, photos, autographs and such.

o Don't talk with them about their on-field performance. They have coaches for that.

Presence –

• Because the chaplain is given entrance to places most people cannot go and thereby comes by information that most people don't have, I asked Walt about how to handle this privilege. His answers follow:

o Moments of crisis are particularly important for the chaplain to be available to the team or individuals. He mentioned the in-season death of a player and the respect that he was shown by the club as they flew him to be with the team.

o It's important to protect the players and the club with the "inside" information you may have. Do not share information like this:

Injuries

Personnel at practice

Salaries

Contracts

Trades

Agents

Who the Christians are on the team.

Who attends chapel or Bible studies.

o Be very careful with any information you post on facebook, twitter, in emails, in blogs, ministry newsletters, public talks or on your web site. Don't betray this trust.

Strategies, Methods and Resources –

I asked Walt about the most effective strategies, methods and resources he has used in his almost forty years of ministry, and he listed these:

o Serving people

o Chapels

o Prayer

o Bible studies

o Devotionals

- Chapel service points of emphasis –

o Arrange the time and location as directed by the head coach or manager.

o Prepare guest speakers

Don't act like a fan.

Don't bring guests with you.

Don't talk about yourself. They don't need to hear your high school sport stories.

Bring a Biblical message. Remember, this is their weekly worship service.

Be very time conscious. Stick with the time allotted to you.

Former players and coaches are often the best for this because they understand the culture and its values.

o NFL teams do their chapels separately.

o MLB teams do their chapels separately.

• Prayer points of emphasis –

o Prayer is modeled in the Bible study.

o Prayer is offered by the chaplain and players at chapel.

o Prayer takes place in a prayer circle at the conclusion of chapel.

o Prayer is done in the locker room before taking the field.

o Prayers are said on the sideline with players as they request it.

• Bible study points of emphasis—"Teaching the Scripture has always been what I have stuck to and has kept the men coming over the years. I cannot emphasize that enough."

o Weekly meetings are best.

Coaches Study

Players Study

Couples Study

Game Day Chapel

o Verse by verse studies work very well. Walt's Tuesday study, now in its 30th year, is on its third trip through the entire Bible.

o Walt uses an inductive Bible study method and

develops his own study guides. His studies are not necessarily directly tied to their sport experiences.

    o Emphasize Matthew, Mark, Luke, John, Acts, and Romans.

    o Allow the group studies to prompt opportunities for individual meetings with players or coaches.

    • Devotional points of emphasis –

    o Walt has distributed thousands of copies of the devotional periodical, "Daily Bread."

    Summary –

Walt Enoch has influenced the lives of countless men, women and children throughout his almost forty years of service with the professional sports community in St. Louis, Missouri. He has also shaped the ministry of many men and women who also serve sportspeople around the world through the sharing of his experiences, values and points of emphasis as detailed above. We would do well to learn from our mentor and the vanguard of such effective ministry. Thanks Walt. We can hear our Lord greeting you, "Well done, my good and faithful servant."

Chapels for Visiting Teams

Occasionally I have an opportunity that I tried to apprehend for a number of years. I am privileged to lead a baseball chapel for the visiting team of Sunday's college baseball game, the finale of the weekend series. I prepared a handout for each player in attendance. It is identical to the one I used for our team that same morning, except for the team specific information and photo. It contained an excerpt from my devotional book, *Heart of a Champion*, a prayer from, *The Competitor's Book of Prayer* (adapted to baseball), and some contact information for me and for the new FCA Director in the visiting team's community.

This is very common in professional baseball as Baseball Chapel (http://www.baseballchapel.org) has the home team chapel leader conduct chapels for both the home and the visiting teams. They are usually done consecutively in each team's dugout or in another convenient area for the players.

In years past, I have arranged for chapel speakers for visiting college football teams. Either I would speak with them, or I would arrange for a trusted friend and colleague to speak with the team. I have also done this with visiting women's basketball teams when they come to our community to play our university's team.

Many of our colleagues in other settings have done similarly, but I would urge you to consider the opportunities that may be at your hand. It took a few minutes to research the head coaches' names and email addresses, and to then send an email offering to lead a chapel for their players. Of the four I emailed, two responded, and only one agreed to arrange a meeting room for his players. It may be that the simple arrangement of a chapel may spark interest in the visiting team's players or their coaching staff for having a sports chaplain to serve their team. It could lead the players to investigate FCA or another ministry on their campus. It could lead to some investigating the claims of Christ Jesus. It could simply be a moment of encouragement for a team battling toward the end of a disappointing season. I'll aim to be faithful and will trust the Lord with the results.

Please consider taking a little time, a little risk, and the discomfort of walking into uncharted waters to serve selflessly and to love extravagantly.

How to Serve People:
Values

Listen

One of the most important but easily overlooked qualities that enables us to be most effective is to listen well. In an evaluation meeting with our university men's basketball head coach, among many other questions, I asked him what the players most valued from my time with them that season. He said, "You listened to them. You let them talk." While that seems very simple, it was also very important to me. As I thought about this later I gained greater understanding about the value of listening to sportspeople.

In the world of sport, the coaches do lots of talking and very little listening. In collegiate sport, the NCAA places a limit of twenty hours per week for the coaches to work with their players. The coaches work countless hours each in evaluating video, developing scouting reports on upcoming opponents, brainstorming game plans, meeting together to strategize and when they finally get with the players they want to communicate and to download all this information to them. They're trying to squeeze hundreds of hours of information into twenty hours of video review, training and practice. Lots of talking and very little listening by the coaches.

It daily becomes increasingly clearer how important the skill of listening well is to my role as a sport chaplain or character coach. The players simply need to process some of what they've been learning, their frustrations, their concerns and more. I can be the listener for them. Simply repeating their questions, restating their thoughts, asking follow up questions, sharing a related life story or simply looking them in the eye enables them to communicate their hearts and to perceive that they've been heard, their opinions valued and their ideas respected.

Yesterday's team building session was emblematic of how such listening helps the development of the players' relationships with each other and with me. We were discussing the fifth of six sessions on Coach John Wooden's Pyramid of Success. In particular we were discussing the traits of: ambition, adaptability, resourcefulness, fight and faith. I asked one discussion question about each and welcomed their thoughts in dialogue. Right out of the blocks while discussing ambition, the players whose pre-season ambitions were playing in the NBA or in Europe were suddenly said to be graduation, finishing the season well and playing their best basketball in the post-season tournament.

The team's record of seven wins and sixteen losses certainly has changed their ambitions. Another player commented during our discussion of adaptability, that he had to adapt from being a starter playing twenty-two minutes per game and getting lots of shots, to being a reserve, averaging six minutes and very few shots.

As we discussed faith, I asked, "When does basketball require faith?" Several said, "Right now." In the midst of a disappointing season, some find it hard to go to practice. Others find the travel, training, practice and more to be a terrible grind. One of the seniors, the unquestioned leader and most enthusiastic player on the team, confessed that for the first time in his life his passion for the game was drying up. He was losing the joy of playing basketball and was almost looking forward to the end. This shocked his teammates and me. We followed up with a question about how faith can help restore the joy of sport and concluded our discussion with a challenge to continue to prepare well, to play these last games as part of the process of improvement and to be in position to play the team's best games during the post-season tournament.

We left the locker room after our twenty minute discussion with open hearts and enthused voices. I am sure that was primarily the result of listening to them and encouraging them to be their best. It surely helped to have Coach Wooden's Pyramid to frame our discussion. Please take the time to listen to your players and coaches. Work to improve your listening skills. Don't simply wait for a pause so that you can start talking. You'll open hearts and enlighten minds more effectively if you just listen.

Questions to Ask
Coaches and Competitors

One of the most effective tools I regularly employ in my service of sportspeople is to simply ask questions. I ask questions to draw them into conversation, and then to probe more deeply toward their hearts. Sneaky, huh?

I tend to ask three levels of questions:

1. Questions that evoke facts. I ask the competitor's name, home town, position, uniform number, etc. Mostly facts. Anyone will offer these details.

2. Questions that evoke passion. I ask about the competitor's sporting experiences, and I'm looking for their love for the sport. I am leading them to tell me stories that awaken their passion for sport, team, competition, coaches, etc.

3. Questions that evoke their hearts. I ask about the matters at the core of who they are: values, faith, relationships, events, and other matters that shape their lives from the center.

Please consider this brief list as a place to start with those whom you serve. I hope they serve you well.

Always ask process questions, not results questions. Fans and media only ask questions about results.

1. How is your team developing? Is the teamwork good?

2. How pleased are you with your _____? (Training, practice, hitting, rehab, etc...)

3. How pleased are you with preparations for your next competition?

4. Who among your teammates is doing very well?

5. What are some challenges you have presently?

6. What sorts of situations in your sport bring out the best of your abilities?

7. How well is your team connecting with the coaching staff?

8. When your playing days are over, what do you think you will miss most about sport?

9. What are the moments in your sport that are most difficult for you?

10. Who are your most trusted teammates?

11. When and where are you most fully the person you want to be?

12. What elements of your life in sport are most pleasing to you?

13. What is there about your life in sport that will still be important to you 10 years from now?

14. When you are on the _____ (floor, field, court, track, mat, pitch, etc.), do you feel that God is near or distant? Engaged or disinterested? Pleased or disgusted? Why?

The Christian Sportsperson's Identity

In recent years more and more Christian competitors, coaches, and sports chaplains have become uneasy about the degree to which they have become identified by their most recent performances. They find their emotions, relationships, and even their sense of personal worth to be tracking with their win/loss records, their most recent times, distances, heights, and other measurements of personal performance. While knowing this can't be right, most have no other way to grasp their worth, their value, and their identity as a person.

The culture in general and the sports industry in particular are happy to give an identity to sportspeople. This is usually in an effort to market, to lionize, or to degrade a person for their own purposes. If that's not enough, those in sports media are more than happy to reduce a sportsperson's life to a cliché, a meme, or a sound bite on their evening broadcast, blog, or talk radio show.

We who work in Christian sports ministry will often tritely say, "Your identity should be in Christ," and walk away as if that instantly solves the whole issue. I wish it were that easy. I've been wrestling for years with how to express a better way for the Christian sportsperson to understand and to embrace his or her identity in Christ Jesus. Please consider the following seven points, and I pray the scriptures, each directly addressing identity, inform your heart, your mind, and penetrate to the depths of your soul.

1. I am not identified by slavery to my flesh. I do not need

to obey its every urge or bow to its appetites. Galatians 2:20 speaks to this matter—"I have been crucified with Christ; and it is no longer I who live, but Christ lives in me; and the life which I now live in the flesh I live by faith in the Son of God, who loved me and delivered Himself up for me." I am crucified with Christ; my flesh is as good as dead. I need not heed its screams of desire. I still live, by faith in Christ. My life in Christ is energized by the same power that raised Jesus from the dead. That's power. That's infinitely more powerful than any urge or appetite resident in my body. I am crucified with Christ, and I now live by faith in Him.

2. I am not defined by my performance, good or bad, personal record or disqualification, league championship or relegation. Ephesians 2:10 holds a transforming truth for our lives in sport—"For we are His workmanship, created in Christ Jesus for good works, which God prepared beforehand, that we should walk in them." I am God's workmanship, created in Christ Jesus for good works. Even more, He prepared works before my appearance that I may walk in them. My identity and my performance on the court, the track, the pitch, the ice, the field, in the pool, or the gym now spring from who I am, not what I do. I am God's workmanship. He has done the work, now I just stroll in the works He has prepared for me.

3. I am defined by neither my brand nor my tribe, not by the logo on my gear or the club for which I compete, not by the club's ownership nor even my nationality. My true identity is stated clearly in I Corinthians 4:1-2—"Let a man regard us in this manner, as servants of Christ, and stewards

of the mysteries of God. In this case, moreover, it is required of stewards that one be found trustworthy." Due to my relationship with Jesus, this text says that I am now Christ's servant, thus He determines my value. I am His. Further it says I am a steward of the mysteries of God. This is a privileged position given through relationship, not merit. The Creator of the universe has called me to serve Him and to be a trustworthy caretaker of the mysteries of His kingdom. That's who I am.

4. I am not an outcast, a loner, a free agent, out on waivers, or between teams. I have been chosen for an elite team. We read about our place on this team at I Corinthians 3:9—"For we are God's fellow workers; you are God's field, God's building." I am now God's fellow worker, a part of God's field, a part of God's building. I do not stand alone or isolated. I am not disconnected or cast off; I am part of God's team, His field, His building. I am in community with all those who love Christ Jesus. I am an integral part of what God is establishing in this world.

5. I am not an asset, a liability, a tool, an acquisition, or any other inanimate, dead thing. Romans 12:1 dispels these pernicious notions—"I urge you therefore, brethren, by the mercies of God, to present your bodies a living and holy sacrifice, acceptable to God, which is our spiritual service of worship." I am not a dead sacrifice, lacking will and animation. Rather, I am a living sacrifice with full capacity to make choices, to love freely, and to worship God. I am free to present my body as a living, holy, and acceptable sacrifice. This is my true and reasonable act of worship. I am one who

worships the living God through the presentation of my body as a living sacrifice in sport.

6. I am not an isolated, forlorn, outcast from society. I Corinthians 12:27 reveals our present standing in the world—"Now you are Christ's body, and individually members of it." I am a member of Christ's body. I have a distinct role and a unique function. I am indispensable in value. I am absolutely integral to the function of Christ Jesus' body in this world. I am a member of Christ Jesus' body.

7. I am not defined by my past. Weak or strong, austere or privileged, rich or poor, wise or foolish, stellar or mundane, my identity is not in my past. Colossians 1:27 frees us from the past and its bondage—"to whom God willed to make known what is the riches of the glory of this mystery among the Gentiles, which is Christ in you, the hope of glory." The marvelous, mysterious truth is that Christ in me is the hope of glory. The powerful hope that makes life worth living, gives us significance, and marks our true identity is the daily presence of Christ Jesus' Spirit in our mortal souls. Christ in me is the hope of glory. That is who I am.

I hope that these powerful statements of identity, directly from the Holy Scripture, are used by the Spirit to transform your life, to free you from performance based identity, and to liberate your athletic soul to compete freely. Rest in the assurance that you are complete in Christ, without regard to today's performance, your team's place in the standings, or any other temporal standard of measure.

Community and Purpose

In May of 2018 I was in Vilnius, Lithuania and Moscow, Russia in support of our teammates of FCA Ukraine. While in Moscow, I had a great talk with a young man who is pursuing ministry in ice hockey. He was an elite level young player and then a professional from age fourteen until twenty. As we discussed what he missed most about playing with a hockey team he said, "My teammates. In the summers, when we would go to a summer camp to train and compete, I would come home after the camp and cry in my room. My mother would ask what was wrong with me, and I would reply that I miss my teammates."

For this young ice hockey player, his team and teammates provided community and purpose for his life. After he was passed over for further advancement in professional hockey, he was suddenly thrust into the real world of work, and this world provided neither community nor purpose. He was adrift. He descended into a life of alcohol and drug abuse, crime, and eventually homelessness. In the midst of this downward spiral, he connected with people in the world of crime. They welcomed him, without condition, and gave him a community and purpose for living, nefarious as it was.

While homeless, a man approached him on the street offering a way out of his plight through relationship with Jesus. At first he said no. When the same man offered again, he asked what he had to offer. The man gave him the phone number of a rehab clinic that could offer him food, clothing, and shelter. When he made the call, he was amazed that they would receive him without condition. This new set of friends offered him community and a purpose for life. He went through rehab, staying and working there for four years.

Now well integrated into his local church, married to a delightful young lady (a former professional volleyball player, now a coach), he and his wife began to dream and to pray about ministry in sport. He said, "How many ushers does a church need? Surely there is a way to serve God outside the church walls." They were both looking for a way to share community and purpose for life with sportspeople.

One day he received a call from a man named John McIntosh. John has a long history of serving the ice hockey community. John said, "I hear you are a pretty good hockey player, and I hear you are a believer. Can we get together?" They met, and that launched their journey toward ministry in sport. They are just beginning, but they already understand the hearts, minds, and lifestyles of elite level sportspeople.

We, as sport chaplains, must be increasingly aware of the loss experienced by sportspeople when they leave the organized, regimented, community of their sport. Whether due to retirement, injury, failure, or simply being released from their contracts, sportspeople experience the same loss of community and purpose as did this ice hockey player. We must find ways to bridge that gap. We must find ways to provide community. We must explore ways to help them find purpose for their lives. Please join me in this most important venture.

Don't Act Like a Fan!

In November of 2003 I spoke with Andrew Wingfield Digby, over twenty years the chaplain to the British Cricket national team, and asked him about particular attitudes a sports chaplain should be careful of, and he said, "Never act like a fan." That statement resonated with me and has become a very important part of my approach to ministry in sport.

Let's pursue that a little further by thinking about the actions and attitudes of fans. Let's go one more step and think about why those actions and attitudes are detrimental to our ministry with sportspeople. I'll take the risk that some of us may take offense to these thoughts.

• Fans are only interested in results. They know what the point spread should be for the game and are critical if their team doesn't win by enough points to cover the spread (and to cover their wagers). They give no thought to the processes which lead to the results, nor do they value them.

• Fans wear their team's gear with their favorite player's name on the back. They identify so strongly with that player that they wear his/her name on their backs and often sycophantically endorse every attitude, action and behavior associated with the player.

• Fans seek autographs from players. Sometimes at the most private moments of a player's life, fans will interrupt and demand an autograph. Many high profile players seek some privacy with family and friends only to have fans barging in to get them to scribble on a cap, a scorecard, a ball, an arm or something even more personal.

• Fans want to pose for photos with players. Before, after or even during games fans will ask to pose for photos with players. They have no idea of the mental preparation, the attention to detail and the focus for competition which they're interrupting by asking for the photo. In post-game situations, that may include the processing of the pain of loss and other feelings which have the player at less than his or her best.

• Fans fantasize that they could actually play the game. Hopefully we're close enough to the court, field or pitch to realize that most of us are not even 20% athletic enough or skilled enough to compete with those we serve. A healthy amount of humility is required to work well with competitors and coaches and to keep our attitudes in check.

• Fans criticize players' performances. Sports talk radio, chat boards, bars and coffee shops are crowded with sports fans who are critical of their team's players' performances as measured against their expectations, their salaries or their profile. Worse still are those who become critical of players based on their performance as Christian athletes. They judge the players' lifestyles, their relationships, their tattoos, their hair styles, their behavior on and off the field of competition and the amount of "religious" language they hear from the players in interviews. If they don't perform their religious duty well enough, fans become critical and even question the validity of their faith in Christ.

Sports Chaplain or Character Coach, whatever you call yourself—please don't act like a fan! Rather, invest your life, your heart and your time in the lives of those whom you serve. Share the love of Christ and the communion of the Holy Spirit with them. Rather than seeking anything for yourself, give yourself away. Rather than criticizing their performance, religious, sporting or otherwise, encourage their hearts, and challenge them to be all Christ has called them to be. Value the process of development in their whole lives over the results from the most recent competition, and you'll be on the right track.

Loving Unlovely Sportspeople

In our service of the men and women in sport, not everyone will be lovely and kind. Not everyone will be amiable and honorable. Not everyone will be wise and reasonable. We will certainly be surrounded by some unlovely, crude, mean, selfish, and nasty people. Our sphere of service and influence extends to the nasty as well as the nice. We must care for the obnoxious unlovely as well as the absolutely lovable. How shall we accomplish this? I have some simple thoughts listed below.

1. Purposefully appropriate Christ's love you have received toward others. When dealing with difficult people or with those with whom I cannot connect well, I will pray for the person and set my will to transfer the love I have received from the Lord Jesus to this person. This may seem overly simple, but it is very effective in shaping one's attitude toward the less than lovable in our lives.

2. Make a list of the person's admirable traits and affirm them when you interact with him or her. This may certainly be difficult, but it is worth it. To find a characteristic of the person, to name it in conversation with him, to write a complimentary text message or card, to speak well of that person's character in public, can turn an annoyance into an alliance.

3. Seek an opportunity to serve or to give the person a gift. It's really hard to maintain a grudge or to keep a conflict alive when we are serving or giving gifts to them. The Proverbs are full of wisdom for how one's gift can pacify contentions, and Jesus' way is to love even our enemies.

4. Remind yourself that this person is one whom the Lord Jesus loves. Through decades of leading in summer sports camps, I would challenge our staff about half way through the camp to love the campers (and other staff members), who had grown into annoyances. I would challenge them with this task. "When you see that terribly annoying person, the one who gets on your last nerve, say to yourself, 'Here comes the one whom the Lord loves.' That may be enough to help you control your attitude, to reshape your tone of voice, and to find a way to communicate the same love the Lord has for him or her."

5. Give the person some space. Sadly, not everyone wants to hang out with us. You may be gracious, kind, loving, and wise, but some people will still resist you and may even be antagonistic toward you. Relax. Some people make assumptions about you due to poor relationships with others in your role, with others from your organization, with others in the Church, with Christian family or friends, or they simply don't like how you wear your hair. Give them some space. An opportunity to serve may come along that can crash through those barriers, and you may be the one person on the planet well prepared to care for the person and to extend the love to Christ Jesus in the most appropriate and timely way.

In summary, may I challenge you to love extravagantly and to serve selflessly, the lovable and the unlovely, the wise and the foolish, the amiable and the surly, the gregarious and the grouchy. In doing so, we emulate and honor the Lord Jesus.

Behind the Scenes vs. High Profile

Many of our colleagues serve in rather obscure settings, with almost invisible teams or clubs and with coaches and competitors who are much less than household names. Others of us serve with clubs which are on television every day, with high profile people who are seen daily in advertising of all sorts and whose sporting gear is worn by fans of all ages. Many of us are somewhere in the middle with our service being among "local celebrities," sporting people who have some profile in their communities, but not so much celebrity status across the nation or the globe. While serving in any of these stations, it is wise for us to consider how to manage our own approach to obscurity vs. celebrity.

Some of our colleagues trade on their position and use their favor with the club as a central part of their fund-raising, to obtain outside speaking engagements and occasionally to prop up their own sense of celebrity.

Some of our colleagues serve faithfully in more remote situations where the spotlights and television cameras never even appear. They're not tempted by the allure of celebrity or reflected glory of fame, simply because they never even encounter it.

I'd like to have us consider the tension between serving entirely "behind the scenes" and holding a "higher profile" position as a sport chaplain, a character coach or a sport mentor. These are in no particular order, but I hope they spur you to contemplation and wise decision making.

- A higher profile in a community makes it somewhat

easier to do fundraising because people will associate you with their favorite team, institution, community, etc.

• A higher profile can help one build a platform for ministry in a community from which one can gather volunteers and other ministry partners to further your ministry goals.

• A higher profile in a state school (USA) can raise scrutiny from prying media members seeking a controversial story, university officials with conflicting agendas, lawyers with an axe to grind, and others who could jeopardize one's freedom of service.

• A higher profile can cause those one is serving in the club or team to question his or her motives. "Is he here to serve us or to build his "brand?"

• A higher profile is perceived by some as indicative of self-promotion, betraying a self-centered attitude.

• A couple of simple scriptures which can help us check our attitudes and inform our hearts are these:

o Proverbs 27:2 "Let another praise you, and not your own mouth; A stranger, and not your own lips."

o Proverbs 27:21 "The crucible is for silver and the furnace for gold, And each is tested by the praise accorded him." Praise, celebrity, fame and public honors will certainly test our hearts to their core. Some of us will pass and others will fail this test.

Let's live wisely in this tension. Understand that the alluring nature of fame and celebrity can afford us some things which will enhance our ministries, but they can also serve as traps which can seriously hinder as well.

Here is Joy

A couple of weeks in the fall of 2013 were among the most rewarding of my many years of serving sportspeople. The annual process of college football coaches being fired and hired included a number of my friends. For most of them, this year has been better than usual. A couple of the personnel changes have been particularly beneficial to some of my coaching friends.

My son sent me a text message informing me that the head coach of his university's football program had just been relieved of his duties with two years remaining on his contract. He also asked if one of my coaching friends, now a defensive coordinator at a larger program, might have interest in this head coaching position. I told him that I wasn't sure, but that I'd pass the information along to him. Moments after sending a text message to the coach, he replied asking what I thought of the situation and what my son thought of the job. I replied and connected him with my son. They corresponded, and then my son sent me a link to the school's application site. I sent the link and another comment to my friend, and he replied, "Thanks. I will apply tonight."

A couple of days later the coach called me saying that he had received a call from the school's athletic director and that he was very impressed. He said that if he had a real chance at landing the job, he'd get another call to appear on campus for an interview. The day he was expecting a call arrived; he received it and scheduled the on-campus interview. On the day of the interview the coach called me in a moderate panic. His flight from one part of the USA to another had been delayed five times due to weather, and his window for arriving at the campus interview was closing quickly. He asked if my son could get a proposal printed; I assured him he could, and connected them. Later in the evening, proposal in hand, he interviewed with the athletic director and knocked it out of the park. We traded text messages early the next day, and he expected to hear if he got the job by the end of the week.

A couple of days later, my wife and I both received a text message from the coach's wife informing us that he got the job, but we needed to keep things secret until the Dec. 18 press conference at the university. We were thrilled and almost burst from keeping such great news as a secret. My wife, son, and I all decided to be at the press conference and were beaming with pride to see the inauguration of our friend's next step in his coaching career. More than that, it was the next step in the fulfillment of God's purposes for his life.

The new head coach was excellent in his press conference, his personality shining in its truest essence, and he was very gracious in his remarks about those who had invested in his life. After the completion of the interview, we stayed and waited for the media to finish with him, for other friends and colleagues to visit with him, and then we spent some invaluable face to face time with the coach and his wife.

Our relationship with this coach dates back to 2001 when he arrived with a new staff at our university. The relationship hit a new gear when he asked me after practice one day, "Rog, who's speaking at chapel tomorrow?" I replied with the person's name and a little about him, to which the coach replied, "I'm thinking I ought to pray." I chuckled and said, "Yeah, coach, you ought to pray," thinking he meant to pray in general. In a couple of seconds I realized that he meant he wanted to pray during the chapel. I hurriedly amended my comments and said, "Oh, you mean tomorrow. I will set you up in a perfect spot. Watch me, and I'll call on you." He said, "Okay," and I began to consider the best possible moment for him to take the biggest spiritual risk of his life. I could not let him fail in this moment. Time for chapel rolled along, and I queued the coach for his prayer, and he nailed it. From that moment I began to nurture what I could see as a growing faith in Christ Jesus.

I began giving him books to read. I formed a Bible study for the coach and included a couple of my dearest friends who happen to be influential businessmen in our community. I encouraged him and his wife to attend an FCA Coaches Camp, and they returned transformed as a couple. A few weeks after the camp, I had lunch with the coach's wife. She said, "When he and I got married seven years ago, we thought, 'If it doesn't work out, we'll just get a divorce. No big deal.' We're not happy with that anymore." I said, "What would you like to do?" We then began to discuss and to plan for a marriage vows renewal service for the two. In mid-January, during the recruiting season, the coach's wife and I had arranged for a chapel just off campus with candles and music she had programmed in her iPod. The coach thought they were going out for a steak, but they came to the chapel. I was waiting in the candlelit chapel, and we renewed their vows of marriage, now with the Lord Jesus intimately involved. A few weeks later I was privileged to visit them and their newborn daughter as she was arrived appropriately on Super Bowl Sunday.

We were sad when most of that staff left us in 2007 for a new opportunity, but we were excited for them. We stayed in touch as we could, though separated by 300 miles and even spent some time together at that same FCA Coaches Camp, this time with a toddler. Remarkably, they had become financial supporters of our ministry, and for that I am very thankful. At the end of the 2010 season, this dynamic staff of coaches had yet another opportunity, and they took it. The coach and I talked over the phone about whether he should stay or go with the others. We both knew that his ambitions were to be a head coach, and we agreed that staying and entering a new network of coaches could be the best avenue to his goals. He took the risk and stayed for another year, just long enough for his own new opportunity to be the defensive coordinator for another team in the same league. He did this excellently for two seasons and that performance made him a great candidate for this new opportunity to become a head coach.

As all that was going on, two of our coaches were also being interviewed for the same head coaching spot at another university. I sent them each the same encouraging text messages, assuring them of God's favor and wisdom for their careers and families. I spoke to one of them shortly after his on-campus interview was completed and as he waited on a flight home. He was thankful for the prayers and assurances. Early the next day we learned of his appointment to the position and today we learned that he's taking another of our fine, young coaches with him. We are again sad to lose them but excited to see what the Lord has for them in their new roles.

All of these stories, situations, the excitement of new opportunity, and the grief of losing valued colleagues are testament to the value of long-term relationship building and commitment across distance and time. The richness of reward in days like these make the temporary inconveniences and pain of loss seem terribly insignificant. Here is joy.

Sports Ministry and Celebrity Culture

One needs only glance at almost any daily newspaper or turn on the television to nearly any channel to encounter one of the most pervasive, and I believe destructive, elements of popular culture in the USA, the western world and beyond—Celebrity Culture.

We are flooded daily by information which we neither need nor even desire. We hear about the latest celebrity break up or hook up. We read about the newest "It Girl" or "Sexiest Man on Earth." We are suddenly aware of the exploits of people who are seemingly famous for being famous, unencumbered by personal achievement or strength of character. Celebrities of dubious distinction are emblematic of this wave of media inundation and the growing need to fill air time with some sensational story about just about anything lacking substance or significance. The USA has reached new lows in this regard as we even create celebrities ex nihilo. "American Idol" is the most obvious example of this self-absorbed, self-perpetuating celebrity machine.

A quick reading of Acts chapter 14, verses 8-23 will provide a biblical example of celebrity culture in the Apostle Paul's day. At first (verses 8-18) the crowd sees Paul and Barnabas as idols to be worshiped, and in the next (verses 19-23) they are objects of derision to be stoned to death. It is the same crowd of fickle people. We are just like them, but we use mass media to assassinate people rather than stones.

Sadly, we in the world of sport are not exempt of this

culture and its insidious drive to make celebrities of those whom we serve and love. Professional sportspeople are easy and often willing participants. Their flesh is gratified and their wallets are often fattened by the process as they sell their dignity, honor and even their relationships with team and family to this foolish industry. Their privacy is laid on the altar of popularity and Q ratings, which they trust will result in the growth of their "brand," further resulting in greater profits from endorsements, appearances, publishing and more.

We who serve in ministry roles with people in sport walk a fine line between wisdom and foolishness. We swim in a river of powerful currents which can easily pull those whom we serve, and even our ministries toward a tragic drowning. We sometimes trade on the public profiles of those whom we serve and that is a real issue to be faced. Some of our ministries in sport were founded on the principle that just as high profile sportspeople use their popularity to sell shaving cream and beer on television, they could speak of their love for Christ and thereby "be used" to grow the Lord's Kingdom. Such strategies are perilously close to the edge of manipulation and prostitution of the people we claim to love.

One of my colleagues who serves very faithfully with a number of high profile Major League Baseball and National Football League players has a very wise approach to this issue. I asked him sixteen years ago when we were both new to sports ministry about his policy re: requests for players to make appearances at area events, schools or fund raisers. He said that he never makes such requests of active players because he's more interested in serving them than in asking them for favors. He said, "If every time they see me coming across the clubhouse, they think here he comes to ask me to do another talk, I forfeit my opportunity to lovingly serve them and to impact their lives with the Gospel." He gets it! We must not forfeit our ministries of love and service in order to trade on the celebrity of the player with people in the community and even with the donors who fund ministries.

It seems to many that the high profile, celebrity player owes something to the adoring public. It's counterintuitive for us to prefer to keep our relationships with such players and coaches private and to not drop their names at every turn. It's even seen as selfish or snobbish by some when we protect those whom we serve from the provocative paparazzi and the ogling eyeballs of television cameras. To protect the player, to withhold information given in confidence and to value the coach's privacy is still the right thing to do.

Let's be the ones who love without thought of return. Let's love coaches and competitors without reservation and without posing for the cameras. Let's help them find a side door to avoid those who would trade on their sudden celebrity and help them see their true value in relationship with Christ rather than in the number of magazine covers for which they pose.

How Does One's Spouse Enhance His or Her Ministry with Sportspeople?

Where are the opportunities for a spouse to enhance a sports chaplain or character coach's ministry in a significant way? Across my more than twenty-five years of such service, my ministry has been greatly enhanced by my wife in several ways. Let's consider some of the possibilities.

• A spouse can be a tremendous complement to one's service through serving sportspeople in the home. In my case, my wife is tremendously gifted in hospitality. She is an excellent and creative cook, thus part of our service of sportspeople includes having them in our home for breakfast, dinner, dessert, or just snacks. As we host meetings or individuals in our home, the hospitality provided by my wife really sets the stage for my service. Her service makes mine better. If she was not willing to have people "invade our space" it would be much more difficult to serve, and the setting for some of our most effective service would be lost.

• A spouse can add perspective to one's service, due to his or her personality, experience, and giftedness. As most couples are, my wife and I are much different in terms of style, temperament, and giftedness. I am an extrovert; she is an introvert. She serves very naturally; I have to think about it. She is intuitive about people and their motives; I am much more likely to judge things by their appearance. I trust her intuition about people and their motives. We compare notes about situations, and her counsel leads to better decisions.

• A spouse can be a valuable anchor to a sports chaplain's

busy life of travel. Sometimes a sports chaplain's life may include travel with teams, to conferences, to training events, or other travel opportunities. In my case, I love to travel, but my wife does not. Some spouses love to travel with their busy sports chaplain husband or wife, but others would prefer to stay home. My wife, after forty-two years of marriage, does not want to tag along with me, just to have me work all the time, and leave her to hang out in a hotel room. "No, thanks," she says. The benefit to me is that when I travel in my sports chaplain role, I am able to be 100% on all the time. I spend no time thinking about pleasing her as we travel, nor adjusting to her speed. I am able to be my intense, extroverted, deeply engaged self with total freedom. Whether your spouse likes to travel with you or not, he or she may be a tremendous asset to your service.

• A spouse can be an effective oasis for one's consuming life with people of sport. In our roles, we often take on the stress, concerns, pain, successes, and failures of others. This can certainly wear one down, leading to fatigue and other effects upon our hearts. A wise, loving spouse can help distract us from the busyness and secondhand pain we bear. My wife keeps me engaged in our extended family, helps me see other people in our community, and enables me to serve some of the people behind the scenes of the sports world. She volunteers in the equipment room with that staff during football preseason and then on game days. Her care for and personal connections with these people affords me unique opportunities to serve this often-overlooked team of selfless people.

These are just a few of the variety of ways a spouse can be a tremendous complement to a sports chaplain, a character coach, or a sports mentor. I am reminded of the proverb, "He who finds a wife, finds a good thing, and obtains favor from the Lord." I have certainly found a good wife, she is very good, and I have obtained great favor from the Lord. I pray that you find or have found a good spouse, and that you find similar favor from the Lord.

How to Serve Processes:
Values

Questions for Contemplation

Coach Joe Ehrmann's influence in the coaching community of the United States cannot be overstated. *Season of Life*, by Jeffrey Marx is a book about Joe and his pilgrimage from an abusive past to a transformational present and future of coaching at Gilman School in Baltimore, MD. Joe's book, *InSideOut Coaching*, is among the best books on coaching that I've ever read. I constantly share its principles and practices with coaches in my sphere of influence.

I'd like to adapt and apply some of the questions Joe uses in training coaches with us today. Joe's questions are: "Why do you coach? Why do you coach the way that you coach? What does it feel like to be coached by you? How do you define success?" Excellent and probing questions, all.

I would like to have us consider these questions:

1. Why do you serve as a sports chaplain or character coach?

2. Why do you serve the way that you do?

3. What does it feel like to be served by you?

4. How do you define success?

Take some time to contemplate these questions and to even write down your answers. They can become defining characteristics of your further service.

I would like to make some direct and challenging comments about each question.

1. Why do you serve as a sports chaplain or character coach? If you are serving as a way of obtaining access to the team, to gain privilege, or to enhance your public profile, you are doing it badly.

2. Why do you serve the way that you do? If you are serving thoughtlessly, without considering the needs and the preferences of those being served, you can do much better.

3. What does it feel like to be served by you? If those you serve are feeling manipulated, condemned, or simply annoyed, you should consider changing your approach.

4. How do you define success? If your measurement for success is attendance at meetings, you may be terribly disappointed. If your measurement is conversions or baptisms, you may become quite manipulative. If your definition of success is more about long term faithfulness than immediate results, you are on the right track.

Please join Coach Ehrmann and me in asking some difficult, probing questions of yourself. Contemplate these ideas to analyze and adjust your service of the men and women of sport toward life transformation and faithful service of Christ Jesus.

Timing

Another of the important qualities for sports chaplains and sports mentors is a sense of timing. The ability to be at the right place at just the right time is both serendipitous and strategic. We can stumble onto such timing on occasion, but we should also choose the times and locations which best facilitate our ministries with coaches and competitors.

• One should know when to speak and when to keep quiet. Nothing is as annoying as the person who can't be quiet when the moment requires silence and reflection.

"Even a fool, when he keeps silent, is considered wise; When he closes his lips, he is considered prudent." Proverbs 17:28

• One should think carefully about when to be present with the team. For your sport, is it more advantageous to attend practice or competitions? Is it better to be with people prior to or after a contest? Is your presence more helpful after losses or victories? There are surely some situations which better lend themselves to conversation and open hearts.

"Oil and perfume make the heart glad, So a man's counsel is sweet to his friend." Proverbs 27:9

• One should know when to leave people alone. Some people really want to be alone after wins, others after losses. Some value privacy in pre-game preparations while others are very social. Some of us can really get on the nerves of those we seek to serve simply because they feel smothered by our presence at the wrong time.

"Do not forsake your own friend or your father's friend,

And do not go to your brother's house in the day of your calamity; Better is a neighbor who is near than a brother far away." Proverbs 27:10

• One can make a tremendous impact upon people when we say the right thing at just the right time. When you hear encouragement, challenge, affirmation or direction in your heart for the player or coach and you deliver it in the appropriate moment, it is immeasurably valuable.

"Like apples of gold in settings of silver Is a word spoken in right circumstances." Proverbs 25:11

Let's consider the when and where of our ministries. Let's plan wisely to be present in the most advantageous places and times to serve well. Let's also be willing to act on a hunch, an intuitive thought or to answer a random request to visit a player, to hang out with a coach or to show up at the training room, hospital or funeral. We may find our timing is perfect, and we're speaking words of life to starving souls.

What About Your Service as a Sports Chaplain Will Matter in a Hundred Years?

What about your service as a sports chaplain will matter in ten years, in twenty, in one hundred years? What do you do, how do you impact lives, and whose lives are affected strongly enough that your service of them will have long lasting benefits? Let's think about this challenging set of questions.

What about your service as a sports chaplain will matter in ten years? What you taught and modeled for them about success in life can have this sort of effect. When people see your approach to work, how you engage with people, your study habits, and other life skills, they can be significantly influenced for a good period of time.

What about your service as a sports chaplain will matter in twenty years? I would assert that what you taught and modeled for them about God honoring relationships have a strong effect for at least this long. As they observe your loving interaction with your spouse and children, they will be directly affected in a great way. What you teach them about relationships with teammates, coaches, support staff, people of the opposite sex, sports officials, and their opponents on the field of competition will shape their lives for decades.

What about your service as a sports chaplain will matter in one hundred years? What you taught and modeled for them about the person and work of Christ Jesus, that will matter after you and they are all dead, buried, and mostly forgotten. The clear and direct communication of the gospel of Christ will make an eternal difference. Your introduction to faith in the Lord Jesus can break generations of curses, foolish lifestyles, and condemnation that has been a millstone around the necks of many.

Whether your term of service with people in sport is a few weeks, a few months, a few years, or even a few decades, make investments in their minds, their hearts, and their lives. There will be fruit from your faithful service. It may appear in ten years, it may be most evident in twenty years, and it may be most strongly effective in one hundred years. Pray to the Lord of the harvest that He may send more workers into His field, this field, the field of sport.

Cultural Preferences vs. Scriptural Mandates

The longer one is in the Church, the more one is enveloped in its culture, both Christian culture generally and specifically the culture of the local church one attends. There are cultural shifts within any particular church's culture, some seen across decades, others across weeks, and still others that move glacially slowly across centuries. This is equally true of parachurch ministries, but an extra layer of corporate business culture is added to the church culture that defines these organizations.

Whatever the nature of your church or parachurch culture, we must see it clearly enough to keep its cultural preferences distinct from genuine scriptural mandates. To rephrase, we must hold tightly to scriptural mandates, and more loosely hold to our cultural preferences. Let's not confuse the two. Let's also understand which ones are worth fighting for and which are not even worth an argument.

Cultural preferences relate to matters like:
• musical styles, hair styles, clothing, and tattoos.
• jewelry, architecture, language, and   Church polity.
• educational issues, sport, technology, art and icons.

Scriptural mandates are much more important, far less fuzzy, and much more demanding (short list):

• A new commandment I give to you, that you love one another, even as I have loved you, that you also love one another. By this all men will know that you are My disciples, if you have love for one another." John 13:34-35

• So, as those who have been chosen of God, holy and

beloved, put on a heart of compassion, kindness, humility, gentleness and patience; bearing with one another, and forgiving each other, whoever has a complaint against anyone; just as the Lord forgave you, so also should you. Beyond all these things put on love, which is the perfect bond of unity. Let the peace of Christ rule in your hearts, to which indeed you were called in one body; and be thankful. Let the word of Christ richly dwell within you, with all wisdom teaching and admonishing one another with psalms and hymns and spiritual songs, singing with thankfulness in your hearts to God. Whatever you do in word or deed, do all in the name of the Lord Jesus, giving thanks through Him to God the Father. Colossians 3:12-17

• And you shall love the Lord your God with all your heart, and with all your soul, and with all your mind, and with all your strength.' The second is this, 'You shall love your neighbor as yourself.' Mark 12:30-31

You and I, our families, our churches, our parachurch ministries, our friends, our enemies, and everyone else will have their cultural preferences. Wonderful. Let's not allow those preferences to separate us from each other. Let's certainly not let them compromise our commitment to the scriptural mandates to love God, to love our neighbor, to put on hearts of compassion, kindness, humility, gentleness, and patience. May our hearts, full of Christ Jesus' Spirit, permeate and transform each and every culture we inhabit, one heart at a time.

Economy of Opportunity

After over fifty years as a follower of Christ and 20 years of vocational ministry, I think I'm beginning to understand our Lord's Economy of Opportunity. Across those years and across several continents I have seen hundreds if not thousands of ministries which are "needs driven." Those who lead the ministries, either a part of local churches or parachurch ministries, identify the "felt needs" of a particular community, then seek to meet them as a means of expressing the love of Christ Jesus or as an avenue to sharing the Gospel. Noble goals both. However, such a focus on needs can occasionally obscure the recognition of genuine opportunity the significant impact which comes along with it.

Jesus was very familiar with the needs of people and dealt properly with them daily. He also seemed to value opportunity even more highly. Please read the following passage, and listen for the moment when opportunity trumps need.

John 12 (The Message) Six days before Passover, Jesus entered Bethany where Lazarus, so recently raised from the dead, was living. Lazarus and his sisters invited Jesus to dinner at their home. Martha served. Lazarus was one of those sitting at the table with them. Mary came in with a jar of very expensive aromatic oils, anointed and massaged Jesus' feet, and then wiped them with her hair. The fragrance of the oils filled the house.

Judas Iscariot, one of his disciples, even then getting ready to betray him, said, "Why wasn't this oil sold and the money given to the poor? It would have easily brought three hundred silver pieces." He said this not because he cared two cents about the poor but because he was a thief. He was in charge of their common funds but also embezzled them.

Jesus said, "Let her alone. She's anticipating and honoring the day of my burial. You always have the poor with you. You don't always have me."

Did you hear it? "You always have the poor with you. You don't always have me." It is always the right thing to care for the needs of the poor, we always have them. We do not always have the remarkable presence of Christ at a particular moment of greatest impact. This is opportunity, and this is why it outweighs need in the Lord's economy. Bethany was certainly well populated with poor people, and I'm sure Lazarus, Mary and Martha were generous toward them, but they were not Mary's focus on this day. She anticipated Jesus' death and burial and was ready with an extravagant gift of love and respect.

For us who serve the men and women of sport, there are every day, regular even mundane tasks of ministry. There are constant needs for those whom we serve. It's always right to meet those needs. However, there are occasional, even rare moments when opportunity makes its presence known. Sometimes our moments of opportunity come to us in crisis, as it did for Mary. We would do well to follow her lead and to recognize the opportunity, to marshal the resources, to prioritize the time, to risk being misunderstood and to extravagantly express love and respect.

When our ministries are driven by needs we can easily

become consumed by the need, the needy and the constant urgency to meet the daily needs. Sadly some of the most compassionate and gifted leaders and servants in Christ's kingdom become overwhelmed by the needs and have their hearts numbed by the constant pain and distress of the needy. In such a condition they are also desensitized to the presence of opportunity as it arrives. Opportunity may be gone in a week, a day, an hour or maybe even in a minute. As soon as it appears, it is suddenly gone and with it the chance to make significant impact.

We all have some people around us who resemble Judas in this passage. No matter how much wisdom there is in our value of opportunity, they will criticize and complain about waste and misappropriation. Don't worry about it. Jesus has your back, and He says, "Let her (him) alone. You always have the poor with you. You don't always have me."

Miracles are Wrapped in Mundanity

Miraculous moments are wrapped in daily mundanity. We must embrace the latter to experience the former.

When we read the Bible, we are amazed at the miraculous works of God through people like Moses, Elijah, Elisha, Samson, the apostles, and certainly by Jesus. What we often overlook is the daily mundanity that envelopes all of those miraculous moments. Not featured in those stories are the daily tasks of gathering firewood, building fires, removing ashes, preparing food, cleaning utensils and dishes, taking out the garbage, and all the other mundane, ordinary, and essential elements of daily life. They are there but are harder to see.

If we measure ourselves by the miraculous moments and wonder where they are in our lives and ministries, we can get pretty depressed. However, if we can embrace the mundanity of our daily existence and grasp the certainty that our heroes of the faith had to wade through similar daily tasks, we can find courage and affirmation.

I would challenge you to embrace the ordinary, mundane, and even boring parts of your life because it is in the midst of such days that the power of God appears to transform lives. Your life and the lives of those you serve can be marvelously changed by the unexpected appearance of Christ's lovingkindness. Expect Him to meet you in the most unexpected places. He lives there.

Sports Clichés to Avoid Using

As we serve the men and women of sport, the words we use should be purposeful, grace-filled, loving, and helpful. There are a myriad of sports clichés which don't fit the previous description and that we should avoid using. Some of them follow.

"It's just a game." This cliché simply diminishes the value of every hour of training, every year of achievement, and every deep longing in the heart of a competitive sportsperson. Please don't insult them by using this cliché.

"If you ain't cheating, you ain't trying." This would seem obvious, but many who participate in sport think it's not wrong if one doesn't get caught. They equate breaking the rules with maximum effort to compete and to win. Let's not use this language, and let's not encourage its accompanying attitude.

"Second place is the first loser." This is the crass, foolish, younger brother to "win at all costs." It is blunter and adds the label "loser" to anyone who doesn't finish first. Let's not fall prey to this foolish attitude which diminishes the value of everyone who competes but doesn't finish in first place.

"The officials stole that one from us." If we would confess, most of us have harbored this sentiment, even if it's not been expressed openly. Too often we ascribe less than noble motives to officials, think they're fools, or worse. If one really understands sport, he certainly knows that there are far more mistakes and errors committed by the players and coaches than are ever committed by the officiating crew. Most games are won or lost by the players, not the umpire, linesman, referee, or judge.

"You deserve this _____ (fill in the blank)." This thought has taken the USA captive over the last five years. It has polluted our sports culture with entitlement and foolishness. Parents, sportswriters, broadcasters, pastors, and even chaplains can be heard uttering this ridiculous phrase related to wins, starting positions, awards, contracts, playing time, leadership roles, coaching jobs, and more ad nauseum. Sport is the ultimate meritocracy; we win because we earn it, not because we deserve it. At each higher level of competition, it becomes more so. I am stunned at the players who arrive on our university campus and in our sports teams who seem to think that showing up is good enough. They have grown up so entitled that they assume that having arrived here is equivalent to achievement. They think they deserve to win and to be awarded just for being present. We must not feed this monster.

"God gave us this win." Please don't say this unless you're also willing to say, "God gave us this loss." Why would God give you this win? Does He hate your opponent? Does God think your team is holier than the others? Does He like your uniform colors or logo? Let's give this matter more prayerful consideration than comes with the flippant use of this cliché. "With the Lord on our side, how could we lose?" This is similar to the previous thought, but just as foolish. I have heard this more times than I'd like to recall. Usually uttered by well-meaning Christian sportspeople, it is a clumsy attempt to give glory to God for a victory. It would be much better to simply express one's joy and thankfulness for experiencing God's presence during competition and to thank Him for the opportunity to compete with an honorable and excellent opponent. We are foolish when we ask the Lord Jesus to take sides in a sporting contest.

There are surely many other clichés which are unsuitable for our use and unworthy of the Lord Jesus' representatives. Let's contemplate the power of our words and work diligently to find language to serve the men and women of sport with our tongues. We can have a profound impact upon their experiences in sport when we wisely speak, "the very words of God," as described in I Peter 4.

The Source of Joy

During the days of 17-20 September, 2018, I was in Havana, Cuba to train 100+ men and women as sports chaplains. They were very hungry to learn, and we spent two full days discussing how this role of ministry can be of greatest effect in Cuba. We wrapped up the training by praying for their Cuban and FCA ministry leaders then commissioning them all into service as sports chaplains.

At the end of the trip we took a ride to the Jose Marti airport. My colleagues and friends, Eric Anderson, Alex Roque Martinez, and I were discussing the source of joy for people's lives. My contribution to the discussion, now expanded, follows.

It is my observation that the closer one is to death and dying, day to day, the simpler life is, and that life requires fewer entanglements to have joy in living.

Inversely, the more remote death seems to be, daily living requires more stuff to produce a sense of joy, and one's life becomes increasingly more complex.

When asked, "What brings joy to your life?" my friends from the USA usually trot out a list of creature comforts, foods, drinks, or electronic devices. Their daily existences require a massive amount of support, both emotional and electronic.

My friends in the more impoverished and daily perilous nations of the world simply say, "Jesus." Their relationships with the risen Lord supply all the joy necessary to navigate their precarious journeys through life with abundance in their souls.

As I have walked with USAmerican friends and family through battles with terminal disease and the immediate prospect of death, they begin to apprehend the simple and unencumbered joy experienced by our less prosperous global brothers and sisters. They too can reply, "Jesus", when asked about their source of life-giving joy and fulfillment.

Let us join them. Let's unclutter our lives. Let's protect and clarify our springs of joy. Let's reject every rival to Jesus' centrality as our soul's river of living water.

"Keep in Touch."

One of the values I learned from my mentor, Fred Bishop, is to maintain long-term relationships, even across the globe and for decades. He did it by making long trips by car and by writing post cards by hand. He has since graduated to email and social media. I have marveled at the way he was able to stay in touch with people, to pray for them, to encourage them, and to be encouraged by their development as men and women who love Christ Jesus. Below are some of the ways I have found to do this and the results I receive.

I maintain relationships with former players (college football, basketball, baseball, softball, professional baseball) via a number of channels:

• Email—I have nearly 700 people on my weekly devotion list and send them out each Monday morning.

• Text messages—I send a daily verse from the Proverbs to baseball players who have come through our club.

• Social media—I employ both Twitter and Facebook, with a strategic approach, in maintaining contact with players from the past. On Twitter, I post links to our daily devotional site, in English and in Spanish. I also tweet or retweet items I believe could be of interest to those in my Twitter network of 1,300+.

• Face to face meetings—Collegiate sports programs have occasional events like homecoming that welcome former players back to the university, and these are perfect for reconnecting with players from past years. These face to face meetings deepen the relationships that can be further maintained at a distance.

I stay connected with coaches in similar ways:

• Email—Many coaches who have come through our university are also on my Monday devotion list.

• Text messages—During the college football season, I send messages to dozens of coaches for whom I have numbers. I send a prayer, an encouragement, a scripture, a congratulatory note for a big win, or a conciliatory note after a bitter defeat. I always aim to encourage and to inspire.

• Social media—A number of the coaches from our network also follow us on social media.

• Face to face meetings—The American Football Coaches Association holds an annual convention, and I have attended it each year since 2005. I attend not because I am a football coach, but because thousands of them are there. Rather than chasing all over the USA to see them, I can meet them at this event and reconnect very well. There is a similar event in Champaign, Illinois for high school football coaches and there are doubtless similar events for coaches of most other sports. Find a way to get there and to engage the coaches.

I stay in touch with sports chaplains around the nation and the world as well:

• Email—this weekly email is my primary attempt to share what I am learning and often the excellent strategies, methods, and ideas of others.

• Text messages—I have a group of numbers in my phone that are for college and high school football chaplains. I text message these weekly with scripture, prayer, and/or encouragement. I will also send individuals a text message related to particular situations, crises, or opportunities. I also use text messages to promote monthly conference calls for sports chaplains and character coaches.

• Social media—I promote the monthly sports chaplain conference calls via Twitter, and each one is automatically repeated on Facebook.

• Face to face meetings—Events like the PowerUp Sports Ministry conferences, FCA's annual Sports Chaplains Conference, the AFCA convention (for American Football), and other events are excellent opportunities to see a number of our colleagues, to share a cup of coffee, a meal, and to compare notes.

I firmly believe that the Lord puts people in our lives for specific purposes and our responsibility to Him for them does not end simply because their career paths have led them away from our communities. Especially now, when our communities can be held in our hands, electronically, via our smart phones. We can maintain influential, redemptive relationships with countless individuals by very simple and time efficient methods. Please join me in extending the Lord Jesus' love, encouragement, challenge, and instruction by any and every means at your hand.

How "Spiritual" or "Religious" Should My Service Be?

It is amazing to observe the wide variety of styles that we employ in our service of the people of sport. Some of us approach our service like a member of the coaching staff. Others seem more like a pastor who roams the dugouts, sidelines, and locker rooms. Still others are evangelists, without apology, seeking opportunities to share Jesus in any moment. There is certainly room for one to develop his or her personal style of service, but just how "spiritual" or "religious" should our service be?

While speaking with our university's play by play radio announcer earlier this year, he remarked, "I have never heard your work described as religious." I replied that I was glad; rather than being religious I would prefer to be faithful to my calling from God. I think what he meant was that I don't communicate in religious clichés, nor do I imply that going to church services with me is the height of Christian devotion. My way of serving people in sport is to speak in the language of their cultures, rather than importing church culture into their worlds. It is not heard as religious, but it communicates clearly and respectfully.

Some of our colleagues employ the super-spiritual language that fits their church environment as they are on the practice field. While that makes the chaplain stand out as distinctively different, it also creates some distance that many will not even try to cross to connect with him or her.

We may do better to think about our service of sportspeople by focusing on the core of our message, rather than the language in which it is wrapped. Rather than simply spouting the clichés, buzzwords, and illustrations we hear on the latest preacher's podcast, let's find ways to communicate that truly transform the hearts of those we serve. More than religious, such communication is truly spiritual and speaks life into the lives of sportspeople.

Patient vs. Pushy

The tension between being patient or being pushy in my role as a sport chaplain is constant. I regularly wonder if I'm being patient enough with people or if I would simply push a little harder, I might see more immediate results. Am I being too passive with this one? Am I coming close to being manipulative with that one? Should I be patient or pushy? I probably lean toward being more patient after over twenty-five years in this role. Let's consider some of the aspects of each.

• To be patient is to be respectful of the process God is using in drawing people's hearts to Himself.

• To be pushy may be to manipulate rather than to trust God's grace to lead.

• To be patient is to steadily appeal to people to follow Christ Jesus.

• To be pushy is to emotionally appeal to people to love God, now.

• To be patient is to communicate that trusting Christ is very important.

• To be pushy is to communicate that trusting Christ is very urgent.

• To be patient is to trust the Spirit of God.

• To be pushy is to trust one's evangelistic method.

• To be patient is to affirm the importance of relationships based on trust.

• To be pushy is to affirm the importance of relationships based on compliance.

• To be patient is to focus on long-range results which are

hard to quantify.

• To be pushy is to focus on immediate results which are easy to quantify.

I would encourage you to prefer patience to pushiness. Though you may squirm sometimes thinking, "If I had just pressed a little harder, he would have prayed." you'll not be as likely to alienate those whom you serve. If you patiently wait for the Lord to draw them, He'll bring them to you at just the right time, and the wind of the Spirit will blow through your life and regenerate theirs. Jesus knew this and practiced it with Nicodemus in John chapter 3. Give it a read and then listen for the wind of the Spirit. "So it is with everyone who is born of the Spirit."

Present vs. Prominent

Many people who seek the role of sport chaplain or character coach see it as a place of prominence in their community. Some believe that being attached to the high profile team or individuals in their sporting fantasies allows them a measure of reflected glory, and that would enhance their standing in the eyes of others. While this could in fact be true, it is also quite selfish and could carry a number of unintended consequences. If our hearts lean toward prominence we'll seek opportunities to be very visible in the media, we'll seek out television cameras, and we'll ask to be put in the team's media guide or on the web site. Some of these situations come to those who are not even seeking prominence.

Prominence seems to reward us for our role with the team, especially when the team is winning and enjoys the favor of the community. However, when the program is surrounded by controversy, shrouded in scandal or crushed by losing, prominence takes a less favorable turn and can bring shame to all those associated with it. Be careful. Watch your attitude and your hunger for fame. Being prominent is not always helpful to your ministry aims.

Being present with the men and women of sport, especially in the situations which are out of the spotlight is a wise and powerful aspect of ministry for character coaches, sport mentors and sport chaplains. While lacking the glitz and glamour of the press conference and the post-game interviews, simply sitting with a player prior to and after his knee surgery has an immeasurable impact upon your relationship with him. Talking quietly with the coach in her office about resolving conflicts among her coaching staff does not do much for your public profile, but can be of tremendous value to everyone related to the team. Feeling the grief and loss with a player whose father was just murdered, a thousand miles from where the player is in school, is neither fun nor immediately rewarding. Meeting with a young player who is homesick and contemplating leaving the team and quitting school to discuss his options as you drink a cup of coffee at the corner coffee shop doesn't feel all that spiritual, but could impact the trajectory of this young person's life and his family for generations to come.

Presence is a powerful force. When we walk in the room, onto the pitch, across the floor, or step into the dugout, we carry the living, active and powerful presence of Christ Jesus with us. His Spirit inhabits our every moment, and by our simply being there He catalyzes the process of redemption. Before we think of anything clever to say, before we gesture or assume a holy posture, He is acting in the hearts of those we serve. It is the Lord's work to draw men and women to Himself and to nurture their lives in relationship with Him. The great news is that He'll often engage us in the process if we will simply choose to be present with them, more than we choose to be prominent before others.

Your presence is dynamic and revolutionary because Jesus has made you that way. Show up where the men and women of sport are, and you'll find your prominence is really in the Kingdom of God. That matters eternally. The local, regional, national and international media, not so much.

Process over Results

In the fall of 2003, in Athens, Greece I was chatting with Andrew Wingfield Digby of the United Kingdom about sports chaplaincy and as we wrapped up our conversation, I asked, "Are there any other pointers you would share with sports chaplains?" He looked me in the eye and shook his index finger while saying, "Don't act like a fan!" I have repeated this advice on five continents since hearing it many years ago.

As I have contemplated Andrew's statement across the years and have sought to grasp its significance, I have arrived at one value in particular. It is to value process over results in all interactions with people of sport. No matter if it's a twelve-year-old baseball player or an eighty-five-year-old coach, my approach and my conversation is always about process and never about results. Fans only care about results—wins, losses, championships, pay raises, being fired, new contracts, or resignations. To make matters worse, sports media members usually ask the same sorts of results oriented questions, simply broadcasting the same attitude to thousands or millions of listeners, viewers, or readers. The sportspeople are normally either defensive to such conversation or they simply answer in a string of clichés with little to no value or insight.

I prefer to engage sportspeople in terms of process. I ask questions about practice, training, rehab sessions, weight training, player development, personal development of the coaching staff, etc. I ask questions like these: "How pleased are you with this week's practices? What does your upcoming opponent do well? How do your team match up with them? How are things going for (player's name)? What about this team pleases you most? Who is leading well on the field/pitch/court/track? How is your team developing?"

I never ask questions like these: "Are you going to win tonight? Are we going all the way this season? Will we be better than last year? Why didn't you win yesterday? Why are we losing so much? Should I bet on you or against you this weekend? (Obvious, I hope.) Do you think my chapel talk today will lead to a win? Are we going to be champions this season? Who is the best player in your league? Why don't you win championships anymore? Will we beat _____ (rival team) this year? Is this year's team as good as the _____ (great team from the past) team?"

Sports fans see everything about sport in the simplest form possible: results. Sportspeople, those engaged in the daily processes of sport, understand their lives are much better understood and experienced in terms of process. We will connect better with them, we will understand them better, we will communicate with their hearts better if we lean into chatting about process and run away from foolish discussion of results.

Results How Long to Wait?

   One of the constant battles many of us face is the conflict in ourselves between results and processes. How can we measure results? What would we measure? How do we account for timing? How long should it take for results to be evident? How hard should we push for measurable results vs. how patient should we be in allowing processes of evangelism and discipleship to accomplish their work?

   I will not presume to answer these questions for you, but I will take the risk of sharing my approach to such thorny issues. After over twenty-five years of serving in this ministry, mostly in a university sports environment, but also serving among high school coaches, and minor league professional baseball, I have found that the most satisfying, lasting results take several years to develop. It may be due to my relational approach, which values long-term relationship over short-term programmatic strategies, or it may be due to my more Calvinistic than Armenian approach to spiritual development, but for whatever the reason, I see most results over five to seven years.

   The usual reaction to that statement is, "I don't have that many years to be engaged with these people." My reply is always, "Neither do I." I am usually afforded a four to five year window with a player, occasionally longer with a coach. I have found that it is reasonable to observe real, significant, growth in a person toward a relationship with Christ and development of his or her life in Christ in those years.

   Even better, if we build our relationships deeply enough, our influence with these athletes and coaches lasts beyond their days in our sporting programs. Many times, the result of our ministry with sportspeople becomes evident years after they have moved on to another program or are out of the sport. Two such occasions, both being Facebook Messenger messages received in January of this year, are detailed below.

"Hey Roger, It's DJ. How ya been? Also was wondering how I could get my hands on one of your daily devotional books?"

"Roger, I wanted to reach out to you to thank for giving me your prayer devotional, *Heart of a Champion*. I won't lie and say that I've even looked at it since you gave it to me. I have recently, over the last year, started my relationship with God, and through his will he has allowed me to keep your book at a close distance until the time was right. I started the devotional yesterday. I thank you for reaching out to me in a time I didn't trust God and providing a tool to strengthen my relationship with him. I hope all is well with you and your family!!"

The first message was from a former college football player. He has been gone from our program for over two years. During his years with us I had no thought that he was paying any attention at all. I was stunned to receive the message, and was thrilled to send him the book he requested and another one to boot.

The second message was from a shortstop who played for the professional baseball team I serve. He played one season for us, six years ago. I have had limited contact with him since he left the club and is out of baseball. I saw him briefly last year at a celebration of that team's league championship. I was thrilled to hear of the seeds sown in his life through conversations around the batting cage, candid conversations about relationships, Baseball Chapels on Sundays, and occasional attendance at Bible studies, have come to full fruition in a new, growing relationship with Christ Jesus.

May I encourage you with a simple thought? The Lord is not in a hurry. He calls people, and he carries them into relationship with Himself. We have a part to play in that process, but we cannot make things grow. Let's commit ourselves to serving the Lord's purposes in the lives of those we serve. Let's trust the Lord Jesus to produce the results. Let's trust Him to produce fruit that remains, regardless of the timing.

Service vs. Superiority

In the world of sport, the centrality of competition leads to constant comparison and to alternating feelings of superiority and inferiority. Everyone involved in sport can tell you his or her record, ranking, standing in the league, etc.... These are always in comparison to others. Those on top feel superior simply because their performance has been superior to the others. While this is a regular part of the sports world's economy, it is also a terrible trap for those of us who serve as Christ's representatives in it.

If we, while serving the teams at the top of our divisions, conferences or federations, bask in the achievements of our teams and take on an air of superiority, we stand on the brink of terrible foolishness. Our attitudes are in jeopardy and our ability to serve well is in danger. If we find ourselves making comparisons between ourselves and others who serve teams at the other end of the standings and infer that our position in the rankings is due to the effectiveness of our chaplaincy, we are simply deluded.

Christ Jesus' way of leading was to serve. See John chapter 13 for a graphic example of how the greatest leader in history led his followers and how he challenged them to lead in His absence. A strongly held value for service of others prevents one from making foolish comparisons and keeps feelings of superiority at bay. It's really hard to project an air of superiority while picking up trash after practice.

One's attitude is kept in check more easily as he performs the tasks no one else wants to do. We are infinitely more likely to please the Lord while serving quietly and consistently across seasons of winning and losing than when we capriciously ride the wave of success with the highest profile team available. Make the conscious choice to serve, to take the lower place, to eschew the privileges afforded the superior and you will keep your heart in its proper form.

Let's be mindful of the Apostle Peter's injunction to his friends, "...and all of you, clothe yourselves with humility toward one another, for God is opposed to the proud, but gives grace to the humble." Let's choose service over superiority and thereby consistently reflect the heart of the Lord Jesus in the world of sport.

Shall I Pray for Success?

One summer I received a call from a man whose son was playing in a baseball tournament and working out in a series of showcases in the pursuit of an offer to play for a college team. I have known his daughter, who played golf at our university and attended our Fellowship of Christian Athletes meetings. The father and I had only met face to face one time. He called as he was trying to discern whether it was proper to pray for his son to be successful. We had a great chat, and a number of the ideas we discussed are below. Much of what I told him was that it depends upon how one defines success. We chatted a couple more times during the summer as the process moved along and they contemplated opportunities.

I greatly respect John Wooden's definition of success: "Success is peace of mind which is a direct result of self-satisfaction in knowing you did your best to become the best you are capable of becoming." John Wooden

In this economy of success, yes, I believe it altogether appropriate to pray for success. In the world of sport's normal economy of success: that I win every time, that I am first, that I am the greatest of all time; not so much.

I always pray for those I am serving to be successful, but I never pray regarding the results on the scoreboard. I pray that they fulfill their highest potential, that they compete to their absolute best ability, that they experience the best of their sport, that they are great teammates, that they experience the Lord Jesus' presence and pleasure in sport, that they find joy and satisfaction as they compete, and more. I believe this is success in sport.

One of the prayers I have written for competitors to pray are below. I believe they are emblematic of this approach to success.

Powerful God of Heaven and earth,

Today's competition will require my absolute best and the same of my teammates.

Please give us to be at the heights of our abilities.

Please enable our hearts to be united.

Please grant us insight and wisdom.

Please infuse us with strength, speed, and endurance.

We would honor You with each and every second of this contest.

In Jesus' strong name we pray,

Amen.

Later in the summer I received notice that the young player had received an offer from an NCAA Division I university to play baseball. The family expressed their thanks for praying with them about the process, and the young man tweeted his thanks to God for the offer. The player's mother said, "This was such a God thing," and promised to tell me the story about how the offer came about. I was pleased that they were seeking God's counsel throughout the process, even more than simply comparing offers, academic programs, dormitory rooms, and team gear.

What's the Problem with Misapplication of Scripture in Sports Ministry?

After having delivered hundreds of pre-game chapel talks, having lived through over twenty-five sports seasons as a sports chaplain, having heard and read many years of post-game remarks by ecstatic players and more recently, a few years of tweets and Facebook posts, I have endured the misapplication of many verses of scripture to sporting situations. More often than not a player or coach is claiming a promise he or she sees in the Bible and hears it as God's absolute guarantee of victory. More often than not, that scripture has nothing to do with such matters. A few of the more egregious examples follow.

Jeremiah 29:11   "For I know the plans that I have for you,' declares the Lord, 'plans for welfare and not for calamity to give you a future and a hope."

The Lord certainly has plans for us, plans for welfare and not for calamity, to give us a future and a hope, but to infer that means we will surely win today (welfare is more than winning), that we will not lose (a loss is not calamity), and that our future is surely the championship to which we aspire is pure folly. Let's take inspiration from the scripture and trust the Lord with the application of His plans and our future. Let's not force our ambitions into His kind intentions.

Ephesians 3:20-21 "Now to Him who is able to do far more abundantly beyond all that we ask or think, according to the power that works within us, to Him be the glory in the

church and in Christ Jesus to all generations forever and
ever. Amen."

This usually begins with the player or coach imagining
his or her highest ambition or most lofty achievement and
then appropriating Christ Jesus' infinite power to its
fulfillment. Surely the Lord wants us to achieve "far more
abundantly beyond all that we ask or think," right? His
power is at work within us, right? It's only for His "glory in
the church and in Christ Jesus to all generations forever and
ever. Amen." Right? Actually this verse is in the context of
the marvelous power Jesus exerts in the Church to blend
Jews and Gentiles into one Church which demonstrates His
grace and wisdom. Let's not try to foolishly appropriate the
Lord's dynamic and holy grace toward our fleshly ambitions.

Isaiah 54:17 "No weapon that is formed against you will
prosper; And every tongue that accuses you in judgment you
will condemn. This is the heritage of the servants of the Lord,
And their vindication is from Me," declares the Lord."

Many of us will recognize the first line of this scripture
from its prominent, raspy, and passionate use during the
games leading up to the Super Bowl of American Football in
2013. Simply reading the remainder of this verse informs the
reader that this is much bigger than sport. While the one
who spoke these verses may find all of this to be intensely
personal, since he was accused and was eventually
vindicated by the court, he is not wise in his use of this verse
related to his team's victories.

Much of sport rhetoric borrows from the vernacular of
war and battle. It's often effective as a motivational tool, but

is more often the catalyst for belligerent and foolish behavior. The implication is that our opponent's strategy is a weapon and surely the Lord won't allow their "weapon formed against you to prosper." This thought fails on several fronts, the most glaring being the presumption that the Lord Jesus would take sides in a sporting competition. Why would God favor your team in this day's game over your opponent? Does your team love God more? How do you know? Do they have more Christians, more holy Christians, more devoted readers of the Bible or did they spend more time in prayer today? How exactly is the Lord supposed to take sides? The whole, presumptuous thought is folly and is the fruit of poorly trained study method and self-centered application of the holy writ.

Philippians 4:13 "I can do all things through Him who strengthens me."

This may be the king of them all. One can see "Philippians 4:13" scribbled on shoes, wrist bands, eye black or elsewhere on sports gear on any given game day most anywhere in the world. Players will infer that this scripture means that they and their team can take on the best team in the nation and prevail. Our team which enters the game at zero and twenty-two will surely overcome our rivals who come in at twenty-two and zero. Of course we can, "I can do all things through Him who strengthens me." This winless team may in fact beat their previously undefeated rival, but it will not be because this verse is true.

The scripture is true, but it is set in the context of Paul's assurance to his friends in Philippi that he could handle any situation, having plenty, being in want, in comfort or in painful trials. A more appropriate application of this to sport would be to encourage our teammates that we can trust Christ's power to carry us along through losing streaks as well as through winning streaks. He strengthens us to handle pain and injury as well as to handle success and adulation. "I can do all things through Him who strengthens me." Pleasant things or painful things, sorrow or laughter, ease or difficulty, Christ's strength empowers us for all situations.

It is not my aim to simply rant about the misapplication of the Bible in sports chapel talks. Our purpose here is to challenge each of us to wisely interpret and apply the scripture to the lives of those we serve so that they see its relevance to their lives, hear the voice of God in their hearts and respond to Him in faith. If we fail to do this in a way that is faithful to the Author's intent, they hear a voice that is not the Lord Jesus, and they respond in presumption, superstition or selfish ambition, none of which are even remotely related to genuine faith. Let's be wise in our use of the Bible and allow Psalm 119:130 to be accomplished in our ministries—"The unfolding of Your words gives light; It gives understanding to the simple."

Challenges to Long-Term Success

Across my many seasons of serving the men and women of sport at our university, in area high schools, and with a minor league baseball team, I have noticed the relatively brief tenures of others who have served in similar roles. I believe there are a number of factors that have led to the brevity of their service. Some of those are listed below as challenges to long-term success as a sport chaplain or character coach.

Undue urgency—some of us, especially those who are gifted as evangelists or are driven by numerical expectations, may let our sense of urgency for the Gospel override the depth of our relationships with those we serve. When that happens, coaches and competitors begin to avoid us, actively resist us, or find a way for us to leave the team. Beware an overly urgent approach with people; they will feel manipulated and will believe you're simply using them to accomplish your personal goals.

A utilitarian attitude—this attitude is exemplified by the sport chaplain who tolerates the process of sport; practice, training, study, travel, relationships, and competition, but is committed to delivering his talk. Coaches and competitors smell this attitude like a road kill skunk. They readily perceive that the character coach so motivated is simply using them and it fosters distrust and a superficial relationship. We must move beyond tolerance and fully embrace the whole process of sport if we're to ever win the trust and the hearts of those we serve.

Personnel changes—in most every sport there is a

continual process of change. The coaching staff, the player roster, even the administrative and support staff seems to change constantly. If we fail to build relationships with the newest members of the team or become too nostalgic about those from past years, we stand to find ourselves relationally adrift with no connection to those presently at hand to be served. Ride the occasionally rough surf of personnel changes among your teams and connect as quickly and deeply as possible, even when your friends get fired, traded or waived.

Inflexibility—some of us find ourselves on the outside looking in simply because we will not adapt to new situations. This happens all the time as one coaching staff goes out and another comes in. While we may have had a great relationship with the previous coaching staff, the new one doesn't even know our name and may not even like our ministry. If we're too tightly committed to our way of serving with the previous staff and communicate an inflexibility related to changing methods or strategies, it could alienate the new staff, and we have no avenue of service at all. Rather than committing to methods and strategies, let's commit to principles of service and to people.

Entitlement—this pervasive attitude in our culture (especially in the USA) is a blight upon Christian ministry. If we project the attitude that we are owed something, are due a title, deserve a position with a team, or are entitled to privileges with a sports team, we will find ourselves becoming repulsive to the very ones we seek to serve. Rather that acting like we deserve something, let's seek to earn the trust and develop the relationships which lead to privileges properly received.

I am sure that if we each deal wisely with these challenges to long-term success, we can develop wise, dynamic, and powerful ministries with men and women in sport for years and even decades.

How to Serve Processes:
Professional Development

Professional Development of Sports Chaplains

After many years of serving sports teams and individuals, I continue to grow and develop my ways of thinking, my skills, methods, and resources. I would challenge you to do the same. It is much too easy to fall into serving simply in the routine of last season's way, with last year's methods, and last decade's thinking. It's easy to become a dinosaur. It's hard to stay relevant across decades of service.

Here are some simple thoughts re: a Sports Chaplain or Character Coach's development plan:

• Read and study regularly. Of course, read your Bible, but also read good books on subjects like culture, leadership, sports biographies, applied psychology, coaching, theology, and Christian living. Discover authors or genres that interest you, and dive in deeply. Stretch your mind.

• Experiment and evaluate. Take some chances with new methods of ministry. Risk failure. Ask hard questions in evaluating. Challenge your own status quo. Distribute surveys among your constituents to see what connects well and what misses widely. You may just invent the next breakthrough form of ministry in sport.

• Consult with peers and mentors. Reach out to your colleagues and those who paved the way for you. Ask them good questions and listen. Hear their stories. Perceive their hearts' wisdom. Listen and learn.

• Pray for and about the people of sport. Secure a team roster, memorize it, and pray for them. Develop a system to pray for them regularly. Half of our role is to be the priest to this community. Carry their souls to the Lord via intercessory prayer. Faithfully praying for them will awaken your heart to their needs and to their souls' hunger for the Gospel of Christ Jesus.

• Observe and contemplate. Watch practice and competitions. Watch body language, gestures, facial expressions, and more. These are tied directly to their hearts. Contemplate what each moment, tone of voice, mumble, and comment means. Listen for the Lord's voice regarding each heart you serve. Contemplate, "What would the Lord say to this team, player, coach today?" Tune your heart to hear the Lord's voice. He's speaking. Are you listening?

• Learn continually. However you learn best, lean into that and never stop learning. I read, others listen to audiobooks, others like podcasts, others like online videos, and still others learn best in small groups. Be a life-long learner, and your energy will endure, your soul will stay fresh, and your mind will expand beyond your wildest dreams.

Sports Chaplaincy and the Ten Thousand Hour Rule

In 2016, I attended an FCA Coaches ministry event in my state and marveled at the authority carried by our presenter, the depth of his understanding of the material he presented, and the way the whole room of 100+ coaches were riveted to his presentation. There are dozens of others who are certified to present this material, and many of them do it quite well, but no one carries the same weight of authenticity that we experience when this man is at the front of the room. Why is that?

It's not about the material, they each have the same notes, the same presentations, even the same movie clips. It's not a matter of intellect; each of the presenters have plenty of intelligence, plenty of knowledge, and plenty of capacity. It's not even a matter of personality; there are lots of dynamic men and women presenting this model of ministry. So what is it?

As I drove home Saturday evening, I think I arrived at the answer. It's found in Malcolm Gladwell's excellent book, *Outliers*, I read several years ago. Chapter two of that book is titled, "The 10,000 Hour Rule." Page forty contains this paragraph, "The emerging picture from such studies is that ten thousand hours of practice is required to achieve the level of mastery associated with being a world-class expert—in anything." Daniel Levitin "In study after study, of composers, basketball players, fiction writers, ice skaters, concert pianists, chess players, master criminals, and what have you, this number comes up again and again. Of course, this doesn't address why come people get more out of their practice sessions than others do. But no one has yet found a case in which true world-class expertise was accomplished in less time. It seems that it takes the brain this long to assimilate all that is needs to know to achieve true mastery."

I read that book several years ago and immediately agreed with his premise and the excellent examples in the book. I have also observed it in action in some people I know who are world-class experts in their fields. It was worked out in front of me on Saturday, and I began to apply these ideas to the world of sports chaplaincy.

In my monthly conference calls with sports chaplaincy colleagues from around the USA, I regularly ask, "How long did it take for you to get a handle on this role and to feel like you knew what you were doing?" Most are humble and realistic enough to say that they haven't arrived at that point yet. Wise answer. Let's consider some math and some scenarios about how long it may take to get to 10,000 hours and to achieve world-class mastery of sports chaplaincy.

For this exercise I'll paint a picture using American Football chaplaincy among university teams as a premise.

Scenario A—(much like the schedule of a volunteer chaplain)

Four weeks of preseason practices, 30 minutes at practice x 6 days = 3 hours per week, 12 hours total.

Four weeks of preseason meetings and meals at 1 hour each x 6 days = 6 hours per week, 24 hours total.

Two preseason chapels at 15 minutes each = .5 hours total.

A 12 game season attending three practices per week at 30 minutes each = 90 minutes per week, 18 hours total.

12 game days at 7 hours per week, 84 hours total.

6 travel days at 10 hours per week, 60 hours total.

Total hours per season = 198.5   10,000 hours / 198.5 = 50 seasons to attain world-class mastery.

Scenario B—(Let's suppose you are a staff member and sports chaplaincy is your full-time occupation, working 40 hours per week, 50 weeks per year.)

Total hours per year = 2,000. 10,000 hours / 2,000 = 5 seasons to attain world-class mastery.

In my experience, there are lots of people in Scenario A and very few in Scenario B. In any case, to accumulate 10,000 hours in serving as a sports chaplain will take a very long time. Few of us will invest that much time into a voluntary ministry opportunity. So what's the point?

There are actually several points:

1. Watch your attitude. If you think you have this all figured out, you are probably wrong. Unless you have amassed the 10,000 hours to be seen as a world-class expert in this matter, keep yourself in position to learn.

2. Keep at it. Overnight sensations are never that. Most people who achieve powerfully have toiled in obscurity for thousands of hours, honing their skills, mastering their craft before anyone really noticed. Be that committed to your service and press on.

3. Appreciate excellence when you see it. When you encounter someone who seems to have what all the others pretend to have. Pay attention, ask questions, and learn from him or her. That person has likely invested the time, the effort, and the attention to become as proficient as he or she is.

4. Strive to become a world-class master of your craft. Set your course toward excellence and don't be detoured. Read and learn widely. Ask good questions of those who excel. Find and spend time with wise mentors. Commit to your task and practice purposeful neglect. Set aside the petty distractions and get your 10,000 hours in.

Read

Read. Please, pick up a book and read it. We, as a people group, are not the most literary people in Christendom. Most of us are big on "go and do" and not so big on "read and think." I would like to challenge you to read more. It helps to have a plan, and I am pleased to share with you the sorts of books I read and why I read them. I find them to greatly enhance my service of Christ Jesus in sport, my life as a man, son, husband, father, and grandfather.

1. Read your Bible. "The unfolding of Your words gives light; It gives understanding to the simple." Psalm 119:130 Your Bible will neither give understanding nor light unless you unfold its pages to read. I recommend a simple devotional reading plan, supplemented by more intensive study. I also recommend reading from various translations to keep things fresh and to gather insights from different translators. I particularly enjoy reading The Message translation devotionally.

2. Theology and Christian Living books. There is wisdom and insight to be gathered from these books; get some. I owe a debt I can never repay to the friends I made in my twenties as they introduced me to C. S. Lewis, Francis Schaeffer, Oswald Chambers, John Stott, Brother Lawrence, and other good authors. Later in my adulthood I began reading authors like Phillip Yancey, Eugene Peterson, Os Guinness, G. K. Chesterton, and others. Regardless of your level of scholarship, you and I both stand to learn from these authors.

3. Psychology books. These books help us to think

differently. They help us to understand people and why they do what they do. In 2017 I read, *Deep Work* and found it to be remarkably helpful to my own thinking and personal disciplines. Other books (decidedly non-academic) like *Emotional Intelligence 2.0*, *Man's Search for Meaning* by Victor Frankl, *Mindset* by Dr. Carol Dweck, and *Soul Keeping* by John Ortberg, and several books by Malcolm Gladwell have also been very insightful. My mentor says, "Psychology is a good tool, but a terrible god." Keeping this in mind brings perspective to my reading of psychology books.

4. Sports biography books. These books allow us inside the lives, minds, and hearts of people in the sporting world. Often, these are very insightful and occasionally quite painful to read. Among the best I have read are: *The Man Watching* by Anson Dorrance, *Open* by Andre Aggasi, *Leading* by Sir Alex Ferguson, and several by John Feinstein (not all are biographies, but all are helpful). This is especially true for those of us who find our service of sportspeople a little cross cultural. If you did not grow up as a competitive athlete, you may find the people you serve quite odd. These books can unlock their mentality for you.

5. Leadership books. Whether they want to be or not, sportspeople are leaders. Coaches want to be excellent leaders, but they often don't know how. To read leadership wisdom equips you to serve them well and loads your mind with a bank of knowledge they can access. We are leaders by our very nature. Let's sharpen our leadership swords with some good reading. I suggest these as a starting point:

Heroic Leadership by Chris Lowney, *Leaders Who Last by Dave Kraft, Spiritual Leadership* by J. Oswald Sanders, and *Legacy* by James Kerr. "We are all leading, and we're leading all the time. The question is whether we are doing it well or poorly," is a quote from Chris Lowney's *Heroic Leadership* and it is directly on point.

6. History books. It is of tremendous help to anyone serving Christ to understand the context in which he or she is serving. Reading the history of a team, a club, a community, a region, a nation, a continent, or the entire planet is key to understanding the people and how they view their world. This sort of reading has been transformation to my service when I travel abroad. Reading books on Central American, Cuban, Ukrainian, and Eurasian history were profoundly helpful to the development of ministry in those regions.

7. Culture. These books are of great value as one seeks to ride the stormy waves of societal change. Over this weekend I will turn sixty-one years of age. It would be so very easy to retreat to the culture of the 1970s and to become the curmudgeonly old dude, but I refuse. To have any grasp of societal and cultural changes I must read about it. Books like *Millenials, Hillbilly Elegy, Outliers, Soul Tsunami, A Cup of Coffee at the Soul Food Café*, and others have transformational to how I approach cultural matters.

8. Business Management. If you think strategically or analytically, the authors of these books have something to say to you. Among my favorite authors in this genre are Simon Sinek, Seth Godin, and Jim Collins. Some of my

favorite titles are: *The Starfish and the Spider, Good to Great, Great by Choice, Originals,* and others.

Do yourself a favor, and read a book. Do those you serve a favor, and read a book. Whether you do it old school via paper and ink, or on your portable electronic device (I read on both), read a book. Commit to learning for a lifetime. For what it's worth, I read faster and with greater comprehension at sixty-four than I ever did at twenty, thirty, or forty.

By reading good authors, we welcome mentors into our lives from across the centuries. I regularly receive counsel from John Stott, Francis Schaeffer, C. S. Lewis, Oswald Chambers, Eugene Peterson, Brother Lawrence, and other brilliant men of God who have passed from the earth years, decades, or centuries ago. Read.

Cultivate an Interior Life
of Contemplation

Many, if not most, of us who serve as sports chaplains or character coaches go through life at a rapid pace. We thrive on activity and move quickly from venue to venue to love and to serve sportspeople. One drawback to this sort of lifestyle is that we can become rather shallow, and soon our service becomes a string of clichés and buzzwords.

I would like to challenge each of us to cultivate an interior life of contemplation. To make regular time to contemplate God's will, to ponder on scripture we are reading, to think deeply about important decisions and relationships, is wise and most important. Slowing down to read books, to listen to music, or to simply be still can be very helpful in our more active days.

Don't just go, go, go. Stop, stop, stop. Think deeply. Ponder. Listen. Contemplate. Rest.

Find your best rhythm for such hours, days, or even weeks. Your most effective rhythm could be:

· Absolute silence
· Stillness
· Solitary activity
· Running, biking, or hiking
· Listening to music in isolation
· Study in ambient sound

Sometimes we need to think beyond what to do, but also why?

On a personal note, I brainstorm best when at a sporting event. Hearing the ambient sounds of a ballpark, the smell of hot dogs and popcorn, see the players and coaches, fuels my heart's passions and heightens my soul's awareness of the Lord's voice. To write, however, I need more solitude and concentrated time to hammer out exactly what I want to say.

I take the previously brainstormed first thoughts, gathered at the ballpark, and then compose into final form in a more private, quiet, and solitary place, often accompanied by soul enriching music.

Please take my challenge to heart, and find ways to develop an interior life of contemplation. You and those you serve will be directly benefited by the investments.

Time Management

Time management is a continual issue for those of us who live in the sports world. How to balance work, family, ministry, travel, practice time, game days, study, church, exercise and leisure is a dynamic, daily process, and added to all those factors is the ever-changing nature of our station in life. The proportions of time for each of the above listed matters is drastically different for the twenty-five year old father of a new born than for the sixty-four year old empty nester.

Throughout my adult life, making choices related to time management has been an important issue. In my twenties I didn't give much thought to it beyond, "Do I have enough time to get from work to the ball park in time?" I would leave work at 4:30, be at the ball park by 5:30 for a double header fast-pitch softball game and not get home before 11:30. That all seemed very reasonable to me until I was the father of a two-year-old son, and suddenly time was getting squeezed a little. It seemed like a good idea to prioritize some time for my wife. Goodbye fast-pitch; hello slow pitch. In that game, a double header could be played in two hours. Good move.

In my thirties, after a couple of job changes, I was the father of a son playing two sports at the same time. As I looked at a potential career change with lots of travel and nights out of town, I instead chose to be home more, to play basketball with Jason in the driveway, to have time for playing catch, for playing hockey (complete with facial scars), for soccer games and more. That was one of the best decisions of my lifetime.

In my forties, I had already started my work in sports ministry and was getting my feet on the ground when the Head Football coach asked me to travel with the team to road games. That privilege brought on even more adjustments to my schedule and shifting of priorities. It also came with some criticism and misunderstanding. It cost me every weekend for fourteen to sixteen weeks each fall. I would review my calendar from time to time and find that I had worked every day for several weeks. It was wearing me out. I had to find time to rest, but it was not easy.

Now, well into my sixties, I am constantly budgeting time and making decisions about where to invest my time, my energy and my heart. Not everything weighs the same to me. Some matters are very important, and others are less weighty. I have to prioritize my calendar like any other commodity of great value. Of late, I've been prioritizing time for those who seem to hunger most. Last week I wrote about the economy of opportunity, and this is a major factor in my decision making.

Over the last several years, international ministry and travel has been added to the mix and with it has come an even greater need to budget time wisely. Having become a grandfather radically changed my priorities, and I'm constantly looking for a reason to make the one hour drive to see Addison Faith and Elise Nicole Lipe.

So, how do we manage time? Like it or not, each of us only has twenty-four hours in any day. Some of that is given to sleep (a discipline as important as any), some to work, some to family and the remaining to a wide array of other priorities. The issue is constantly: Setting priorities and holding tightly to them. I would challenge you to live purposefully and to shape your calendar, appointment book and wrist watch by your priorities. Once those priorities are set, write them down, and keep them where you can see them. Tell someone else about them for accountability, and then hold tightly to them.

Each day has the same twenty-four hours, each week, seven days and each year fifty-two weeks. Each life has X years. The X factor is more an issue as I approach sixty-five than it was at twenty-five. Let's follow Moses' wise advice in his prayer from Psalm 90. In doing so we can fulfill the Lord's purposes for our lives as mentioned in Acts 13:36.

Psalm 90:12 "Teach us to number our days, that we may gain a heart of wisdom."

Acts 13:36 "Now when David had served God's purpose in his own generation, he fell asleep; he was buried with his ancestors, and his body decayed."

How to Serve Processes:
Self-Care

Who is Your Chaplain?

One of the items of great interest to me in the book, *Replenish—Leading from a Healthy Soul*, by Lance Witt, is the terrible fact that far too many pastors and other ministry workers are terribly isolated. Too few of us have strong relationships with trusted friends or mentors.

This leads me to ask, "Who is your chaplain?" Who is there in your life to provide the same sort of service that you regularly dispense to others? If you didn't immediately have an answer, this is a problem to be addressed. Who cares for your soul? Who knows you well enough to ask you hard questions about your use of time, energy, and relationship? Who understands your life's pressures, your weak spots, your character flaws, and loves you through them?

Are you close enough to your pastor for this sort of relationship? Have you given him or her permission to enter your life beyond your "public persona?" Is there a friend or colleague with whom you meet often enough to be vulnerable about your life?

Although I am an off the chart extrovert with thousands of acquaintances, there are few people I trust with my life's pains and struggles. My introverted friends may find this even more difficult, but with a smaller circle of relationships. Again, "Who is your chaplain?"

I meet with two men every Tuesday at 6:30 am at a local coffee shop. One of those gentlemen and I have been meeting together for over twenty-two years now. We three have walked together through family health issues, a divorce, a suicide attempt, a remarriage, multiple family issues, financial growth and challenge, joy, grief, and pain. Such is life. We know and trust each other. They are my chaplains.

Once more, I will ask, "Who is your chaplain?" I challenge you to find an answer to that question, and to commit to an enduring and vulnerable relationship with someone who knows you well enough to care for your soul's health. The long-term success or failure of your ministry as a sport chaplain or character coach may be determined by this relationship or the lack thereof.

Burnout Indicator Lights

During the 2019 Fellowship of Christian Athletes Collegiate Ministries Conference in Ft. Worth, Texas (USA), the 100+ attendees received a presentation from Licensed Professional Counselor Kim DeRamus Lareau related to burnout. At whatever level of sport we serve, this is certainly a possibility for sports chaplains and character coaches. Our service can be quite consuming, involve many hours, and a good deal of stress. Kim offered the points below as dashboard indicator lights. My outline of notes taken are below. Thank you, Kim.

As you are driving along in your service of sportspeople, teams, and clubs, please keep watch for these warning lights. If they're flashing at you, please take appropriate action. We need you to be at your best to serve well.

Burnout Indicator Lights-

• Emotional reactions don't fit the related issue. (Greater or lesser)

• Stress related physical symptoms. (Headaches, nausea, etc.)

• Anxiety.

• Depression. (despair & hopelessness)

• Cynicism. (more often in men)

• Difficulty in letting go of perfection.

• Decreased ability to rest or recharge.

• Impacts upon relationships. (Self, friends, God)

• Difficulty setting boundaries.

• Addictive behaviors.

• Secondary trauma. (Second hand)

- Compassion fatigue. (Out of empathy)

Suggestions-

- Ask someone for accountability.
- Make time for deep friendships.
- Be mindful of fitness.
- Practice faith disciplines.
- Recharge your passion.
- Recognize we have limited capacity.
- Seek counseling.
- Make time for a hobby or creativity.

Books:

Boundaries When to Say Yes, How to Say No To Take Control of Your Life by Henry Cloud and John Townsend

Dare to Lead by Brené Brown

Healthy Emotional Spirituality: Unleashing the Power of Authentic Life in Christ by Peter Scazzero

Soul Rest by Curtis Zackery

Didn't See It Coming by Carey Nieuwhof

Solitude, Groups, Crowds, and Family

One of the ongoing, constantly shifting, concerns of my life and ministry is managing the ratio of time spent in solitude, in small groups, in crowds, and with family. I know each is important and even vital to a healthy lifestyle and a vibrant ministry, but what are the proper ratios for each aspect of life?

It would be very tidy to assign twenty-five percent of one's time to each area and to call it done. I cannot do that for a number of reasons. My life is seldom that tidy, being the foremost reason. I believe giftedness, personality type, and season of life, each being other factors in building these ratios. Let's think about these facets of life and ministry individually and about how heavily each one should weigh in the structures of your life and ministry.

Solitude—Each of us would surely say this is an important part of our lifestyle and ministry. To have quiet, private time for reading, contemplation, and composition of ideas is vital. But how much of your day, week, month, and year should this occupy? For me, personally, this is most difficult. Because of being extremely extroverted, easily distracted, and full of energy for activity, I find solitude very difficult. My moments of solitude most often occur while driving my car down the highway. I build one day per month into my calendar for quiet reflection, reading, planning and such, and I usually can make that happen. (Thank you John Stott for the recommendation.) Once a year, I plan and execute a three to four day study retreat where I can be 100%

alone, listen to music, read, write, and plan the coming year. Some of my friends, and my wife in particular, are perfectly happy with hours per day of solitude and quiet. They find it fulfilling and relaxing. I about go nuts in the first two hours! Let's find time for solitude, whether it is two percent or fifty percent of your time will likely be shaped by personality, giftedness, and calling.

Groups—I am sure we would each and all see the need to live and serve in small groups. To interact with people in groups of 4 to 24 is both healthy and builds community in an excellent way. We can know people deeply when we spend time with them on a regular basis, whether focused on study, worship, service, or fellowship. The best groups combine a measure of all four elements.

This is the environment in which I best serve and grow. I seek groups and regularly start new ones. The extroverted among us will soak up the energy of the group and thrive in its life. The introverted among us will likely be drained by the group, and the larger the group the more quickly their energies will fade. If one is an introvert, finding the proper size, content, and focus for group life would seem to be most important. They need group life as much as the extrovert needs solitude, though not necessarily their preferred cup of tea.

Let's find a way to build small group life into our schedules. Let's entrust our hearts to some trustworthy men and women who will care for us in our best and our worst days.

Crowds—I seldom find people who are ambivalent about

crowds. Most folks either love the chaotic movement of a sea of unidentified human beings, or they are intimidated, crowded, and disturbed by the masses. For some the crowd is something to be avoided, while others feed off the energy and emotion felt in large groups of 200 or more people. These people are very comfortable in crowds and don't feel any compulsion to know everyone's name.

I believe it is healthy and even wise to find some time to be in crowds. In ministry, these crowds are like huge fishing holes. In crowds we can meet people new to us, we may find candidates to join our groups, we may find new friends or ministry partners, and we can simply enjoy the unique strength and joy that is afforded those who participate in corporate worship in a huge crowd. No matter our natural comfort in crowds, let's find ways to participate in them and to gather from their unique advantages.

Family—I am sure you have read about this, attended seminars, done the workbooks, watched the videos, and suffered the pangs of guilt offered by so many related to the life of your family. I will not add to your load of guilt and despair. Rather, I would like to have you see family life from a broad perspective. One's season of life should probably be a strong factor in how one prioritizes time and resources related to family.

When I was a young husband and father, we were rather poor and scraped together a living with long hours of work and little recreation time. We spent a lot of time with family because we had no choice. Later, as our careers developed and our son got older, we prioritized time to be with him in his youth sporting activities. It was the right time to invest those hours in practice, driving to and from games, and playing ball at home with him.

As we became empty-nesters, our use of time shifted more toward career development and time with my wife. Now as grandparents, we carve out time to drive the hour and a quarter each way to be with two little girls. We make time for them, regardless of most other factors. Over the years, the ratio of time spent with family was largely dictated by the opportunities at hand for the best expression of love, commitment, loyalty, and investment in those for whom we care most deeply.

Finally, please hear the admonition of one who has made enough mistakes to have some perspective. Please make time for solitude; your soul needs it. The Lord may speak to you in the quiet moment, if you have one. Please seek out and form intimate small groups; you and they need it. The Lord may speak to you through a trusted and loving member of your group, if you are in one. Please find a way to be in a crowd on occasion; your vision needs this. The whole world is not just like your small group, nor like the person in your mirror. Your vision can expand and your hope can be renewed in a healthy, vibrant crowd experience. Please make time for your family, all those around you need it. Your family is a model for the untold number who are watching you. You have a unique opportunity to show all those around you what a Christ-honoring family looks like, warts and all. Love them extravagantly, and the world will beat a path to your door to learn how.

Refresh

Refresh. During an FCA Camp for collegiate student-athletes, I was privileged to facilitate a group for the FCA Chaplains and FCA Campus Ministry Directors who brought the athletes to camp. Rather than have these adults lead the groups for the collegiate athletes, the camp director asked me to lead this group so as to refresh them. I was thrilled to have this privilege.

In one of our small group discussions, we chatted about how their souls are refreshed. We all have our souls worn down by busyness, urgency, disappointment, demands, and the more draining aspects of ministry in sport, but what refreshes your soul? Let's consider what it is to be refreshed and how we may experience that regularly.

Dictionary definition: Refresh verb

• to provide new vigor and energy by rest, food, etc. (often used reflexively).

• to stimulate (the memory).

• to make fresh again; reinvigorate or cheer (a person, the mind, spirits, etc.).

• to freshen in appearance, color, etc., as by a restorative.

Think for a minute about the people, moments, foods, drinks, books, movies, music, and places that refresh your soul. Go get some of that, soon.

The Apostle Paul wrote about how his friend, Philemon, refreshed the souls of people in Colossae at Philemon verses 4-7 "I thank my God always, making mention of you in my prayers, because I hear of your love and of the faith which you have toward the Lord Jesus and toward all the saints;

and I pray that the fellowship of your faith may become effective through the knowledge of every good thing which is in you for Christ's sake. For I have come to have much joy and comfort in your love, because the hearts of the saints have been refreshed through you, brother."

• The prayers of your mentor Do the prayers of your mentor(s) and the mention of them in a letter refresh your soul as they surely did Philemon's?

• Love and faith toward the Lord Jesus and all the saints Does the development of these matters refresh your soul?

• A growing understanding of all we have in Christ Do you find refreshment in sharing your faith as Paul told Philemon to expect it?

• Joy and comfort from love Do you provide joy and comfort to your friends, mentors, and colleagues? If so, you are refreshing their souls.

• Refreshing the hearts of the saints Philemon did this; do you? Who provides that sort of refreshment for your soul? Get some time with them.

You may have thought of refreshing places, foods, and situations. I hope you also thought of refreshing people, groups, and occasions. Expect your heart to be refreshed by nurturing relationships with mentors, with peers, and with those whom you serve. They will stimulate and refresh your memory as to God's faithfulness and goodness. They will renew and cheer your soul. They may even freshen your appearance, your color, and act as a restorative to your whole countenance. Refresh.

Refuel

Refuel. It's likely that you are occasionally feeling that you are out of gas. You seem to be running on empty. Your normal passion and energy seem to be in short supply, but you press on anyway because people are counting on you. You need to refuel. How? What does that for us?

In dozens of years of serving people in sport, I have had a few occasions like that. In most cases it was due to being overly busy, distracted with unproductive tasks, and losing touch with my "Why." In his excellent book, *Start with Why*, Simon Sinek challenges leaders to operate from their "Why," the central reason they do what they do. The people we lead, the people we serve, and those with whom we serve certainly experience "What" we do. They also perceive "How" we do it, but how clearly do we communicate the "Why" that is central to the whole process? The "Why" provides passion, purpose, and long-term direction for our service. Sinek calls this the golden circle, as illustrated here.

What we do, serving the men and women of sport in the name of Christ Jesus, is certainly shaped by How we do it, with humility, respect, compassion, understanding, and other important values. But if our service is not connected with a clearly defined "Why," it will probably not endure for long and will likely wander from a wise and productive path.

If you are running on empty, take some time to contemplate on the Why of your ministry. Why do you do this? For the paycheck? I hope not, as most of us are volunteers. Why then? To apprehend this idea, to write it down, to distill it into an easily expressed sentence, can be a key part of refueling your passions, your energy, and your impact. I recommend the reading of *Start with Why*, as Sinek's explanation and examples of those who do this very well. Refuel.

Rest

Rest. For many of us it is a mysterious, confusing idea. For others it is as elusive as a unicorn. For others it is something we have trouble embracing as our compulsion to work drives us to work more hours, more days, and to leave vacation days unused. Rest. It's important. It's imperative. It's a commandment of God.

A few years ago during an FCA Sports Chaplains conference, a speaker verbally punched me in the nose. He said that, morally speaking, to fail to Sabbath is equivalent to committing murder. Each is a violation of one of God's ten commandments. Ouch. I was immediately and deeply convicted. I had to confess and repent of my ridiculously consuming work schedule that had far too little margin for rest. While still sitting in the auditorium, I opened the calendar in my phone and blocked open every Sunday with a long green bar titled, "Sabbath."

The commandment is stated rather simply, "Observe the Sabbath day, to keep it holy. Work six days and do everything you need to do. But the seventh day is a Sabbath to God, your God. Don't do any work—not you, nor your son, nor your daughter, nor your servant, nor your maid, nor your animals, not even the foreign guest visiting in your town. For in six days God made Heaven, Earth, and sea, and everything in them; he rested on the seventh day. Therefore God blessed the Sabbath day; he set it apart as a holy day." Exodus 20:8-11 MSG

Before you lose your mind about legalism, Sunday vs. Saturday Sabbath, and more, take a breath. Focus on the second sentence, "Work six days and do everything you need to do." The Lord God rested 1/7 of creation week, who are you to think you should not? Sabbath is blessed by God. Sabbath is set apart for God's special use. Sabbath is good for you. Remember Jesus' words about the Sabbath? "The Sabbath was made for man, not man for the Sabbath."

You're probably thinking, "Yeah, but you don't know how much I have to do." That's exactly how I tend to rationalize my failure to Sabbath, to rest. The problem is that when we fail to rest, we remove most of the margin in our lives that allows us to think clearly, to spend time with family, to enjoy life, and to experience God at an unhurried pace.

You're probably thinking, "How am I supposed to do this?" This is the most difficult part of the process, beyond the simple decision to do it. For me, it was a simple choice to schedule for Sabbath. I set a recurring appointment for all day Sunday, each week, forever. However, life is seldom that simple. Sometimes my life requires that I work and/or travel on Sunday. When that occurs, I immediately schedule for rest in that same week on another day. It's a matter of personal discipline. Rest restores your body, mind, and spirit.

Below are some simple ways to build rest into your weekly, monthly, and annual calendars:

Schedule a day weekly for rest. At least one. Most of us have a five day work week. Rest.

Schedule one day per month for quiet and contemplation. (Thank you John Stott for this idea.) Guard that day from busyness. Use it to read, to plan, to contemplate, to pray. Rest.

Schedule your vacation days well in advance and use every one of them. Urgency will pressure you to leave some unused, but if you plan well in advance, you can maximize their effectiveness. Use every personal leave day you are allowed. Rest.

When you embark on your days or weeks of rest, maximize their benefit. Shut down your social media. Silence your phone. Surround yourself with people whom you love and who help you relax. Rest.

The Lord who created us knows how we function best. He says to rest one-seventh of our weeks, our months, our years. (We haven't even opened a discussion of sabbatical years or years of jubilee.) Trust Him more than you trust your Protestant work ethic. Trust Him more than your obsession with your calendar. Trust Him more than your performance based identity. Trust Him and rest, as He did.

Restore

Restore. According to the dictionary, to restore is: re·store—to bring back (a previous right, practice, custom, or situation); reinstate.

To return (someone or something) to a former condition, place, or position. What is there about you that needs to be restored? What about you is broken and needs to be returned to a former condition, place, or position?

Across many years of serving in this role, I have been occasionally broken in various ways. I am often in need of restoration. Relationships get strained and need to be restored, more often than we would like. At sixty-four years of age, I need some occasional physical restoration. I find that my attitude is often a little sideways and needs restoration. How I think about particular issues, people, or groups often needs to be restored.

Regardless of the nature or the degree of your brokenness, find a way to be restored. There are certainly a number of ways to be restored, and I have listed some of the ways I have found to be most effective. These are often a little radical, but they are also very effective.

1. Rest. Brokenness and pain are often the result of fatigue, sleep deprivation, and the loss of margin in our lives. Take some time off, rest, and be restored.

2. Repent. Some of our brokenness is simply due to willful sin and foolish patterns of lifestyle. Repent. Change direction. Stop it. Be restored.

3. Confess. Agree with God and with trusted friends, that your brokenness is sin, and receive God's forgiveness. Read

I John 1:9 again, and again. Be restored.

4. Ask forgiveness. The path to restoring relationships is to ask forgiveness and to extend it to others. Find a way to express your heart, bury your pride, and be restored.

5. Resign. My brokenness is often because I'm over-committed and serving outside my giftedness and calling. Yours could be as well. Resign from such roles and be restored.

6. Refocus. As our brokenness dissipates and our vision clears, we are better able to focus on our calling from God, our giftedness, our strengths and weaknesses. This process of restoration enables us to refocus on wise and God-honoring goals. Refocus and be restored.

These ideas may seem really simple, and they are. Broken people don't need complexity, they need a simple plan to be restored. Please take the time to appropriate one or more of these strategies and be restored. Those who care about you, those who work with you, those whom you serve; we all need you at your best. Restore.

Tips for Your Study Retreat

There has been a good deal of development to the process of taking study and prayer retreats over the few years in which I have employed it. I would like to share with you some of the important factors to study retreats that I have discovered and that I would recommend as you consider scheduling such an event.

Choose a good site for solitude—As I am a terminal extrovert, I know I need this sort of solitude, but I find it terribly difficult. Having a place to study, pray, and to create that is free from distractions is of paramount importance. My son's in-laws own a lake house in rural Missouri, and another friend has a hunting cabin in rural Southern Illinos. They are relatively simple but have enough creature comforts to make them very well suited for retreats. They have no Internet connections, which is helpful to eliminate distractions. The areas surrounding them are usually vacant when I am there, as they are mostly weekend or vacation homes. This leaves me all alone with lots of solitude for walks, sitting by the lake, watching the sun rise or set, and for outdoor contemplation. Choose a site with a strong measure of privacy for your retreat.

Take productivity tools with you—music, videos, books, and other materials that may fuel your creativity and productivity are invaluable for such a retreat. I play music that stirs my heart, and this time I took a DVD of U2 videos for visual images to supplement the music's inspiration. I take my computer for writing. I take my favorite Bible for reading. I take my notebook with a good pen for writing outlines. I take other books that inspire and fuel creativity. Take whatever you need to make you most productive.

Eat, drink, and sleep well—There are probably particular foods and drinks that fuel your creativity and productivity. Take them with you. I take foods that are easy and quick to prepare, so I don't lose a lot of time. I take good coffee. I need a good breakfast to work well, so I am most particular about that meal. I take some simple snacks and drinks. I seek the best place for sleeping and prioritize this as an important part of the process. I find that long periods of concentrated thought, writing, planning, and analysis is even more fatiguing than physical exercise. Be sure to rest well as it will restore your energies for the coming hours and days.

Take a break to let your brain rest—Once I went to the retreat with a good deal of preparation already in hand. I had done some idea incubation for several months, and when I arrived at the retreat I could jump right into writing. Another time, I was not nearly as well prepared. I had hoped to jump into writing, but I had not done the work to be at that stage. That required me to spend eight hours of the first day writing more detailed outlines. I took a break or two during the day to walk, to make lunch, to go out for dinner, and then to sleep overnight. My brain needed the rest to finish the task.

When I got up on day two, I was fully prepared and spent thirteen hours writing. I took mind breaks a few times during those hours, to walk, to eat, to snack, to read, and even to reply to a phone call and text messages. I was able to complete the project with clarity of thought, primarily because I took the necessary breaks throughout the day to rest, to refocus, and to resume the deep work of writing.

Learn how your mind works best and schedule to be at your best. When I first did these study retreats, I used a friend's lake home. It is about thirty-five minutes from my home. It was convenient but maybe a little too close. I could plan the retreat, but it was also pretty easy to cut it short or to simply not go. Another location for retreats is about two hours from home and requires more planning to accomplish.

I set aside particular days well in advance, and I protect those dates on my calendar. I make plans to leave my home in the morning, arrive prior to noon and eat lunch. This is my time for adjusting from the normal, fast paced life, to a slower, more contemplative speed. That process used to take me a whole day, but I can make the shift in about ninety minutes now. I schedule that first day primarily for preparation. I schedule day two for maximum productivity, and I schedule day three for review, editing, relaxation, and for anticipation of returning home and reentering the normal schedule and work.

Please take a day, three days, a weekend, or a whole week for a study retreat. Engineer your environment, your menu, your schedule, and your heart for maximum productivity, amazing creativity, and inspiring contemplation. Your heart and your ministry will be greatly enhanced.

How to Serve Situations:
Daily Life

No Scale of Level

One of the most pernicious and destructive notions in sports chaplaincy is the confusion of level, success, and significance. Many assume, but would not likely state aloud, that ministry at the lower levels of sport (junior high, high school, community college, minor league baseball, lower division football) has less significance and is of lesser value than the ministry taking place at the highest levels of sport (Premier League Football, NCAA Division I, NFL, NBA, MLB). Somehow, we buy into the fan mentality and judge "higher" levels of sport to be more significant. We value the players' "platform" over their experiences and relationships in their sporting communities. I believe this to be a grave error.

I would assert that there is no level of scale in our service of sportspeople. There is no greater value to the ministry taking place among a NCAA Division I SEC Football program that can be found on television every Saturday, than there is with the junior high school, nine-man football team in the most remote corner of Minnesota. The ministry that I provide an independent minor league baseball team is no lesser in significance than that shared with the New York Yankees or Los Angeles Dodgers. There is no appreciable difference in the Lord Jesus' economy.

Faithfulness is the standard. Whether we serve in the obscurity of "less important" sporting communities or live as the presence of Christ in the blinding glare of television cameras at the "highest level" of sport, our standard of measure and success must be faithfulness. The Apostle Paul declared this value in I Corinthians 4:1-2. "This, then, is how you ought to regard us: as servants of Christ and as those entrusted with the mysteries God has revealed. 2 Now it is required that those who have been given a trust must prove faithful."

Significance is the goal, more than success. A focus on success will spend a lot of time measuring attendance at meetings, distribution of materials, funds received, bank balances, and more. Significance is focused on depth of commitment, progress toward faith, development of spiritual disciplines, growth of disciples' faithfulness, and long-term development of Christian sportspeople. Paul wrote to Timothy with specific instruction about the goals of his instruction in I Timothy 1:5. "The goal of this command is love, which comes from a pure heart and a good conscience and a sincere faith." This is the language of significance, not success.

My opinion is certainly biased. The perceived level of the teams, coaches, and competitors I serve varies from mid-major to the very bottom. I see the perceived highest levels of sport from a great distance, usually from the cheap seats or on a television screen. I would like to finish today's thoughts with a strong challenge.

If you are at the "highest level" of sport, guard your heart from the pride of platform. The higher the platform you, your team, your coaches, and your competitors occupy, the greater the peril they must constantly endure. The same spotlight bringing attention to their faith in Christ will shine glaringly upon the weaknesses of their flesh. Give them your best, every time, and faithfully pursue significance.

If you are at the "lowest level" of sport, guard your heart form the pride of obscurity. Your service has great value and must be treated with care, discipline, and diligence. To undervalue your service, to minimize its importance, to neglect those you serve because no one seems to be watching is foolish and not worthy of Christ. Give them your best, every time, and faithfully pursue significance.

Broad and Shallow or
Narrow and Deep?

One of the tensions I experience often is whether ministry initiatives should be broad and shallow, involving lots of people at a nominal level of depth, or narrow and deep, involving fewer people at a much greater depth. One thing is for sure, to expect things to be broad and deep, will only disappoint you.

The second tension comes with the assumption that one can only do one or the other, broad and shallow or narrow and deep. I would like to have you see these as complementary in nature, not adversarial. I strive to do both, with different goals, with different expectations, sometimes with the same groups.

For instance, with the minor league baseball team I serve I do both approaches to ministry with the same club in the same week.

• Broad and shallow—Baseball Chapel on Sunday after batting practice. Everyone may attend, and no preparation is necessary from anyone except me. It takes about fifteen minutes from start to finish. It's very shallow in depth as I am speaking with a wide range of spiritual maturity. Players and coaches attend, only on Sunday home games. That's usually around eight meetings per season (96 games).

• Narrow and deep—Bible study after batting practice on a weekday afternoon. I give each interested player a devotional book and a New Testament (Spanish / English), with instructions that we'll read the devotion assigned to the day of the year and the chapter of Proverbs corresponding to the day of the month. We all do the reading and then once during each home stand, we discuss our insights from the daily readings. Occasionally I'll meet one on one over breakfast with a coach, a team captain, or have a couple of players to our home for dinner. I even played a round of golf with a couple of players on an off-day afternoon.

With our collegiate FCA group, we do both, broad and shallow as well as narrow and deep.

• Broad and shallow—We hold occasional large group meetings in an auditorium in the athletic department. They are designed to draw in people who are less comfortable in a more intimate atmosphere but may find a large group more inviting. It includes some music, video, prepared talks, and time to meet people, all in sixty minutes. Broad and shallow, purposefully.

• Narrow and deep—We also hold smaller group meetings in my home. They are often for student-athletes of any sport, sometimes for a specific team, and occasionally even one on one meetings with a student-athlete who desires some personal mentoring. Much narrower and much deeper.

The big idea to keep in mind in this tension is to understand the nature of your event and to program wisely. Don't set yourself up for failure by expecting a large group with minimal commitment to dive into a deep discussion requiring a lot of preparation. If the group seems broad and deep, speak their language, start where they are, make it convenient, and work to move them forward to greater depth and commitment. In that broad and shallow group may be a few who desire something with greater depth. Help them start another group. If your aim is to provide a study with depth, requiring study away from the meeting, at an inconvenient hour or location, you can't be upset if the attendance numbers are low. You have programmed for narrow and deep; the group will be narrow and deep.

One size does not fit all. Listen clearly to your group and they'll likely reveal their depth and breadth by their choices of location, time of day, subject matter, and frequency of meeting. Move ahead with their desires, challenging them to grow in relationship and commitment. Watch for the outliers in the group and serve their interests. You'll soon perceive how to complement the broad and shallow with the narrow and deep.

Rewarding Moments

In 2013, our Southern Illinois University's football program (American Football) celebrated its one hundred year anniversary of competing in that sport. As a part of the celebration they chose an "All-Century Team" of players and coaches from across that span of time. They chose a number of players from each position and three coaches, totaling eighty-three in all. It was a great weekend and a tremendous opportunity to see many of the players whom I've known over my twenty seasons of serving the team.

That weekend and several occasions since then have led me to reflect on the rewarding moments that we often experience in our roles of service. I am listing many of these below, and I hope they raise your awareness as to such opportunities. There are enough painful moments, days of doubt and frustration, periods of worry and misunderstanding, don't you dare miss the moments of reward. A couple of these per year can keep me in the harness through months of criticism and barrenness.

Phone calls—an occasional call from a player who asks for prayer prior to a job interview or announces the birth of his new baby is warmly received and touches the soul.

Text messages—the brief, direct communication I receive from players and coaches goes straight to my heart when they share news or ask for prayer.

Returning players—at homecoming games, during special events like mentioned above or on any occasion, the smiles, hugs, back slaps, and the stories told between the team chaplain and the players who have gone on in their lives and careers, are priceless.

Weddings—I have been privileged to lead several couples, made up of collegiate athletes or coaches, through the preparations for marriage and their wedding ceremonies. The opportunity to serve them in this way and to help shape their relationships is richly rewarding and a little intimidating in its importance.

Births—for some of the couples whose weddings I have been privileged to officiate, I have also been present on the days their babies were born. To visit the family, to hold their newborn and to be asked to pray for their child is among my life's greatest privileges. I feel like Simeon from the book of Luke blessing the Christ child.

Facebook messages—a few times across the years of my having a presence on Facebook I have been stunned to receive a message from a player from many years past describing the impact of our ministry upon his or her life.

Funerals—this one may not be so obviously rewarding, but to be present when people's hearts are laid open by grief provides us with opportunities to love them deeply and without resistance. Such moments also prompt some vulnerable expressions of gratitude and reflection by those we serve. To walk with them through the pain is worth it when we connect this deeply.

I am sure I could find some more, but I trust this short list of rewarding moments will be sufficient to fuel your imagination for the discovery of similar instances in your experience and even in your future. Let's love extravagantly and serve selflessly.

Privileged Information

As we serve coaches and competitors in the sports world, we often bear the burden of privileged information. People tell us things that the general public, others involved in the team's life, and certainly the media don't need to know. Many people clamor for such information, but somehow we are trusted with it. A brief list of items follows to illustrate the sorts of information we often possess and the reasons for keeping it confidential.

Injuries. During most every visit to a team's practice or training session, at one point I will be chatting with the athletic trainer (physio) and discussing a player with an obvious injury or the rehabilitation process with those in recovery. The big issue here is that if such information is shared with the wrong people, it becomes a factor in shaping the wagers on a contest. We could unwittingly become the person who shapes the betting line in Las Vegas. Beyond that, in the USA, there are laws that normally prevent medical professionals from sharing any information about a patient's condition. To receive such information is a rare privilege which can be easily revoked if we prove to be less that faithful with the privilege.

Relationship problems. We may be sought for advice related to the problems in relationships experienced by players, coaches, support staff, and others. These may be with their significant others, their spouses, their parents, teammates, with their coaches, or with the players they coach. Across twenty-one seasons of service with football, I have encountered each of those at least once. It is wise to be very careful with all such conversations and to not share this information with anyone. To breach confidence with this information could easily shatter the relationships foundational to our service and could certainly feel like betrayal to the one who shared his or her life with us.

Team conflicts. Among competitive people, these are a constant. As people compete for playing time, for leadership roles, and other matters, it's very easy for the competition to result in personal conflicts. There is just as often conflict among a coaching staff due to perceived alliances, personality clashes, comparison of salaries, and more. It is wise for us to handle the information very carefully. We must not take sides and must always seek reconciliation.

Personnel adjustments. The hiring, firing, resignation, retirement, suspension, and other reasons for movement among the coaching staff, their support staff, and administration is of great consequence for everyone involved. We may be allowed in the process before such moves are made. We could have information about a person's firing even before the person being fired. We may have privileged information about someone's impending resignation, and the local media would love to have an inside track to break the story. All such information is precious and must never be shared with anyone. To breach this trust could end one's service with a club or university upon the first violation.

Legal issues. Should we get wind of an impending lawsuit against a coach, a player, our club, or someone else in our realm of service, we must be very careful with this information. We should be moved to pray, privately, and not to share the information at church. Rather than to discuss the merits of the suit with others, we should pray for a wise and just resolution of the conflict. No one benefits from our sharing information about such matters.

Disciplinary issues. As team members violate team rules, we could be called on for wisdom, perspective, or counsel. Across my years a number of coaches have asked my advice related to possible disciplinary matters. Emotion often clouds the judgment of coaches and others who lead in sport, and many will seek the counsel of others who know the people, and understand the situation but are less directly involved. Sometimes that means a call to the team chaplain, the character coach or the sport mentor. As we find ourselves drawn into such a process, treat this privilege with prayer, confidentiality, and wisdom.

Our service of sportspeople will often find us in possession of very privileged information and weighty responsibilities. Let's reflect the Lord Jesus' nature of faithfulness, wisdom, and purity as we handle such precious privilege as it will surely directly affect our relationships.

Compassion

Let's consider another in the long list of necessary traits for sports chaplains and sports mentors—Compassion. It can be defined this way: "Compassion is a human emotion prompted by the pain of others. More vigorous than empathy, the feeling commonly gives rise to an active desire to alleviate another's suffering."

The Bible is full of expressions of our Lord's compassion, and this one is among my favorites:

Psalm 103:13-14 (New International Version)

13 "As a father has compassion on his children,
so the LORD has compassion on those who fear him;

14 for he knows how we are formed,
he remembers that we are dust."

We who serve the men and women of sport must be conscious of each one's background and the factors which have brought him or her to this place. Many are from homes with poor parents, no parents and at least half in the USA come from broken families. We must be mindful of from what they are made—as the Lord is aware that we are made from dust.

We must treat our work with them as a long-term process and not think that we can solve all of life's issues with one simple prayer, a ritual or with a skillful talk. It may have taken twenty years for the knots in the person's heart to be tied, and it may take a while to untie those knots of sin and brokenness.

We must also exercise compassion with coaches, administrators and other adults in the system. Let's be mindful of the pressures, the weight of decisions, the constantly changing factors and the relational dynamics which result in their reactions to people or situations. Many of these people are just as fragile in heart as the youngest players they lead. These adults just have more powerful positions and a more mature appearance.

Let's decide in our hearts to practice compassion as an essential part of our ministries. Let's remember how the people of sport are formed, knowing that they are made of dust, as are we. Let's care deeply for them and thus wisely reflect our Lord's heart toward those who revere Him.

Seasons in Sport

It is the nature of the sport world to divide the annual calendar into various seasons, not Spring, Summer, Fall, and Winter, but pre-season, on season, post-season, and off season. It is helpful for those who serve people in sport to have a strategy for each of these seasons. Below are some brief thoughts about different sorts of initiatives one can undertake in each of your team's seasons.

Pre-season: This is the perfect time to learn all you can about the people on your team. Work to meet everyone who works with the team. Learn the names of players, coaches, and the support staff like physios, athletic trainers, equipment managers, operations people, office staff, strength and conditioning coaches, etc. I would challenge you to memorize the whole roster of players' names, uniform numbers, and hometowns. This is the time to lay the relational foundations for the ministry opportunities that will follow.

On season: This is when you execute the plans you have made, and you work to fit into the rhythm of the team's life. Listen well for expressions of spiritual hunger and seize each opportunity as it arises. Pray for a sensitive heart and wise presence with the team.

Post-season: Should your team compete well enough to make it to a set of playoffs or a post-season tournament, enjoy the ride. Treat this as a new season with unique opportunities and work to help each individual and the team collectively to finish well. Most of the time these tournaments are one-off events, and while each team thinks they'll emerge as champions, only one will. Be very present and self-controlled in order to serve everyone, especially if the team is eliminated short of the championship.

Off season: The easiest thing to do in the off season is nothing. It is far better to use this time to rest, to evaluate, to plan, and to prepare for the future. It's wise to meet with the head coach to discuss and to evaluate your service of the team. Ask the hard questions like: What worked well? What did you like that we did? What did you not like? What would you like to have me do more? What would you like to have me do less? What do you most value from my role? How can I serve you and the team better? Use the information gathered from this meeting to make plans and to prepare for the next pre-season.

The seasonal nature of sport can be of tremendous benefit to us if we'll understand the unique nature of each season and its opportunities to serve and to grow our ministries. The dynamics and rhythm of sports' seasons diminish monotony and enhance our anticipation of the Lord Jesus' movement in the hearts and minds of the men and women we serve.

Serving Wisely Across Gender Lines

Across these last twenty years of ministry in sport, I have had opportunities to serve both men and women. While there are many similarities in my approach, there are some major distinctions as well. I have had over twenty seasons of serving a men's college football (American Football) team, college and professional Baseball for several seasons, and less formal relationships with individual male competitors. I have also served a Women's Basketball team for almost twenty seasons, a Women's Volleyball team, and individual female competitors in Swimming, Diving, and Softball. Let's think together about some ways of serving well across gender lines.

Set wise parameters for your ministry across gender lines. In my ministry with men, as I am granted access to offices, changing (locker) rooms, and such, I feel free to go with few restrictions and no anxiety. In my ministry with women's teams, I am much more conscious of boundaries. When invited into a female coach's office to talk, I do not close the door. I don't walk into the locker rooms, when invited, until someone tells me everyone is dressed. I do not give young women rides home from ministry meetings. I keep our interactions from becoming overly familiar. As relationships build, I am sometimes greeted with a hug, but I am sure to keep them from becoming too intimate. I am careful about the nature of our discussions. I meet with female coaches in public places, never at my home or my office. Setting wise parameters can help keep the relationships on the proper plane and avoid foolish affections.

Wisely define relationships with those you are serving. In the first season of serving a Women's Basketball team, twenty years ago, I was very confused at first. I did not know how to properly to relate to the coaches or the players. I grew up with no sisters, my only child is my son, and I had been married to my wife for nineteen years at that point. I knew how to flirt with women but was pretty sure that wasn't the right thing to do. I had to figure out how to relate to these people. In reading I and II Timothy I understood the instruction he was given to treat the older women as mothers and the younger ones as sisters. I began to see the coaching staff as sisters and the players like daughters. I had to learn from my friends about how to relate to sisters and daughters, but I figured it out. This resulted in a great deal of freedom and a greater sense of ease among them. Defining these relationships in this way helped me to view them properly and to care for them appropriately. It also enabled me to be a "surrogate father" to young women who are often competing in sport, being primarily motivated to please their fathers.

While many in our profession will insist there is no proper way to serve across gender lines, I have found that it is possible to serve well, if one sets proper parameters and wisely defines relationships with those he or she is serving. Whether serving men or women, within your gender or with the opposite gender, let's commit to serve selflessly and to love extravagantly. It's really hard to fail when those are our guiding principles.

A Sport Chaplain's Game Day

This is an account of a normal game day during a college football road trip in my life as a sport chaplain at Southern Illinois University in Carbondale, Illinois.

I am normally an early riser, but even more so during such trips. I will get to bed very early on Friday evening and awaken well before dawn. I'll gather my Bible, iPod, notebook and coffee cup. I'll make my way to the hotel lobby or, weather permitting, outside for some reading, solitude and contemplation of the coming day. I'll take some time for intercessory prayer for each player and coach related to their assignments and personal development. I will also put the final touches on my chapel talk, which I would have drafted the evening before.

I will dress and prepare for the chapel by arriving early and distributing a devotional letter to the team at each place setting for the pre-game meal. I greet the players and coaches as they arrive in the room and then begin the chapel at the head coach's prompting. This is typically four hours and fifteen minutes prior to kickoff.

I will ask a player or coach to open the meeting in prayer and then will begin my talk. It's usually five to seven minutes long and begins with a statement related to today's situation followed by a scripture reading which parallels that situation. A summary of the scripture's main points forms the outline for the applications which follow. I will take my last minutes to apply the scriptural principles to this day's situation, to challenge and to encourage, praying to finalize the talk.

A season of prayer will follow the talk, either by the whole team saying "The Lord's Prayer" in unison or by having different players or coaches pray for the offense, defense, special teams, coaching staff, officials and our opponents. I will finish the season of prayer and thereby conclude the chapel.

After chapel, we will have our pregame meal and a brief talk from the head coach. From there it's back to the room to make final preparations for the trip to the stadium and the painfully long wait for game time. I will make my way from the room to the bus early, and we'll drive to the stadium. I'll often use the time after arrival to review the travel list and to pray for each player on the roster by name. I'll stretch and prepare for pre-game warm up activities. I'll catch and return the footballs kicked by punters and kickers, speak with a number of players, challenging them to lead well and to play their hearts out. I'll often pray with individuals who request it.

After our pre-game warm-up activities are completed, the team will return to the locker room where I'll have the stadium countdown clock on my wristwatch, so the head coach will know the timing. We'll hear a final pre-game talk by the head coach, we'll take a knee and the hands of those near us, and I'll lead the whole team in saying "The Lord's Prayer." We'll then take the field and play the game.

I am the team's "get back coach," meaning that it's my responsibility to keep the sideline area clear for the officials to move freely and for our team to not incur a penalty. I'll also help gather special team units to the sideline according to down and distance situations. At half-time I also keep the countdown clock on my wrist and advise the coaching staff as to the time remaining prior to the second half kickoff. When the game resumes, so do my on-field responsibilities. If we're behind, I'll work to encourage and to inspire a comeback. If we're leading, I'll work to challenge our players to finish well and strongly.

At the end of the game, I encourage our players to treat their opponents with respect as they greet them on the field, and then we gather in the locker room. We'll either celebrate or console each other, depending upon the outcome, and then we'll again take a knee for "The Lord's Prayer." After a final talk from the head coach, we shower, change and exit the locker room for the buses. I meet the players and coaches near the buses and help distribute the post-game meals. I speak individually to them to encourage and to praise their performances, their effort, attitude, etc.

Once the buses are loaded, we travel home, and I listen to music, watch the movie, write in my season journal, or all three. I occasionally even sleep. This is how I spend half of my Saturdays throughout the fall, and I dearly love it.

How to Serve Situations:
Critical Incidents and Crises

Comfort in Chaos

Our service of the people of sport is often mundane and slow. There are hours of standing and watching a practice, long bus rides or plane flights to endure along with occasional doubts about the wisdom of such use of time. At other times we're in a vortex of noise, confusion, anxious personalities, screaming people and indecision. To serve effectively we must find a way to be comfortable in such chaos.

We feel the chaos for a number of reasons, among them is the fact that we're really not in control of most of the situations where we serve. Someone else is running the practice, the competition, the emergency room, the surgery center, the coaches' conference room or changing room. The lack of control feels like chaos.

Another reason for our discomfort is that we're seldom the center of attention. If we're Church leaders, we're probably used to everyone following our lead and our agenda. It feels chaotic when we're not in charge of the timing of the team's activities. We have to become comfortable with that and simply fulfill our responsibilities.

The closer one is to the court, pitch, field or ground at the time of competition, the more the chaos is amplified. While standing on the sideline of college football for over twenty-five seasons has ruined me (I hate to watch games from the seats) it has made me progressively more comfortable with the rush of chaotic-feeling noise and activity which surrounds me and the team.

Let's become comfortable with the chaos which accompanies our world of sport and simply relax. Our relaxed attitude will make us more effective in service, more winsome in nature, and more intuitive in heart with those whom we serve.

Ministry in Moments of Crisis
Big Losses

Let's consider the crisis of big losses. Not a crisis you say? Evidently you've never lost a game to your most fierce rival. It seems you have never been upset by an opponent who was by all appearances vastly inferior. You must have never lost a game at the end of a long string of wins. If you don't feel the sting and crushing pain of loss, you must have never played in a post-season game with hopes of being league or national champions. To those who lose big games, it is certainly a crisis with all the emotions of death.

I remember the pain of a loss after a winning streak of ten straight at the end of a college football (American football) season. Our hopes of a perfect season and our expectations of striding into the post-season and onto a national championship were dashed in the final moments of a closely contested game. I remember the deathly quiet in the locker room and the solemn tone of the flight home.

Just this week I saw the residual pain of our basketball team having lost to a team in our league who had yet to win a conference game. We helped them break their streak and continued our descent into mediocrity. It was a short-term crisis simply because we had to practice the next day.

No matter the circumstance, big losses feel just like crises of greater gravity. The emotions are the same, even if the consequences are lesser. For us who serve the people of sport, our attitude and focus should be the same as it is in injury, illness or death. To empathize, to offer consolation and to lend perspective are all appropriate actions. To attempt to diminish the gravity of the situation by saying such phrases as, "It's only a game," will only result in alienation from the people and in our ministry being marginalized. To say, "Just get over it," to those whose hearts were just crushed by a disappointing loss is similar to making such a trite comment to a grieving widow. Foolish at best and hard-hearted at worst.

If we can maintain a Christ-honoring perspective on life and sport, we can be of immeasurable value to the sportspeople we serve. We can help them see crises, big and small, in the light of God's sovereignty and to trust Him in all circumstances. (I'm writing to myself in many of these lines as I feel the losses of my teams much more deeply than the victories. The pain of defeat lasts much longer than the thrills of winning.) Let's stay in touch with our Lord and thus share His transforming grace in moments of crisis, like losing to _____ (insert the name of your team's rival).

Ministry in Moments of Crisis Injury

There is probably no lonelier place on the planet than the sideline of a field, court, pitch or mat when one has become injured. The game, match or contest continues and the injured is taken to the sideline to deal with his or her pain, blood, unconsciousness, etc. The competition continues, and the injured person is left in its dust.

Suddenly one is watching someone else play his or her position. He or she feels alienated and terribly alone and these feelings are piled upon the pain or shock brought on by the injury. In many sports, especially the more violent ones where injury is frequent and even likely, one's teammates will look at anything to avoid seeing the injured player and dealing with the possibility that they could easily be the next one on the physio's table. This results in even more feelings of alienation.

On one such occasion I was watching a football practice when #43 made a tackle, and then a teammate collided with him, striking him on the crown of his helmet. His spine was compressed, and he suffered the latest in a long line of "stingers." Imagine the pain and shock your arm feels when you hit your elbow's "funny bone." Now imagine that sensation across your whole body. Such were this player's stingers and this day's was no different.

We accompanied him to the emergency room unsure as to whether or not he would walk out. After CT scans and many other tests, a few hours of desperate prayer and a few jokes to lighten the mood, my friend left the hospital sore but walking. The stressful, intense, terribly uncomfortable moments of face to face communication and heart to heart communion deepened our friendship and our common trust in God's grace and mercy.

Ministry in moments of crisis like injury take place in locations like these: on the sideline at practice, in the training room, in the ER, at the surgery center—in the waiting room with parents, children and spouses or in the hospital room with the one awaiting or recovering from surgery, and occasionally in the coach's office during the dreaded conversation regarding the end of one's playing career. Each place is one of terrible dread for the injured, but it can be one where he or she experiences the presence and peace of God when we carry Christ's Spirit in with us.

In these moments I always feel inadequate. I always wonder if I have the right thing to say. I never have "magic words" which can make everything okay. I never think I have done all that can be done. I always have to trust God to be sufficient while I am totally insufficient.

I pray that you run to, rather than avoid these situations. These are the moments when the people of sport need us most desperately. You and I may be the most thoroughly equipped to handle such crises as we condition our hearts by the example of Jesus, the Apostles and the prophets throughout the Scripture. Let's commit ourselves to boldly serve those whom injury has alienated from their sport, their teammates and the singular source of satisfaction many of them know—the field of competition.

Ministry in Moments of Crisis Serious Illness

Through my many years in this role, words like cancer, leukemia, lupus, diabetes, and more have sent shock waves through teams, families and the souls of men and women. Suddenly the rules of life have changed for the players and coaches, and a life threatening disease is the number one opponent for everyone. Thoughts of rivalries, practice plans, schemes and recruiting are immediately "back burner" items.

One such instance was in 2005 when our head football coach Jerry Kill encountered grave illness: cancer. It began with in an incident on the field during a painful, homecoming loss to Illinois State University. Below is an excerpt from my journal for that season.

The whole game was overshadowed by an event in the last thirty seconds of the game. Coach Kill collapsed to the turf and suffered a series of three grand maul seizures as I and others rushed to his side and tried to keep him from hurting himself or others. The ambulance on the scene was on our sideline within a minute, and he was quickly taken to the Memorial Hospital emergency room.

After he was in the ambulance, and the clock had run out, Coach Denver Johnson of Illinois State called all his players up to mid-field where our team met them on one knee. As Coach Johnson was watching the scene develop, I asked him if he would like me to pray, and he consented. We each took another's hand, and I prayed for Coach Kill's safety, his recovery and freedom from long-term effects from this incident. After the moment of prayer, we congratulated our opponents for their excellent play and retired to our locker room.

Once inside, Coach Tracy Claeys did a tremendous job of comforting our players about Coach Kill's condition and directed them to stay in touch with their position coaches for updates. We all took a knee again, held the hands of the men near us and prayed "The Lords' Prayer" together as is our custom.

We exited the locker room to a subdued crowd of fans, friends and family outside. My wife had already left for the emergency room and I soon followed. When I arrived, Coach was already in an observation room, and I was allowed access because the ER doctor wanted to know how the incident occurred. I told her the story with all the detail that I could. As the evening progressed Coach had a series of equally severe seizures in the hospital. The hospital staff continued to increase his medication in order to stop them, but they continued to happen and caused Rebecca and all of us great concern. Pastor Allen Speer and I were there throughout the evening, praying for Coach Kill and doing all we could to comfort the family, while the coaching staff and university personnel gathered to lend support.

Finally after midnight, the seizures had stopped, and he had regained consciousness enough to talk with the doctors. He had a couple of CT scans done, but there was no apparent damage. Around 2:30 in the morning, he was transferred to the Intensive Care department. My wife and I accompanied Rebecca and the coach through the transfer and into his room.

The good news is that Coach Kill is doing well physically, and after a strong run at SIU, he took the head coaching job at Northern Illinois University for the 2008-2010 seasons. After three strong seasons there, the University of Minnesota offered him their head coaching job, and he accepted it. He endured the cancer, surgery, and has come out the other side stronger.

These moments of crisis, the emergency room visits, the nights of sleeping on hospital room floors, the prayers prior to surgery with the coach and his family were the defining moments of my ministry with him, and they are the reason for our continuing ministry with the coach and his team even though they're now hundreds of miles away.

A second instance which illustrates the importance of such moments to our ministries is Coach Lance Irvin's battle with leukemia. As I was watching for ways to serve men's basketball here at SIU, I became aware that Associate Head Coach Irvin was in Barnes Jewish Hospital in St. Louis, MO. I decided to make the two and a half hour drive to the hospital to visit with him. I found the coach in his room as he was in day fifteen of what became forty days in the hospital receiving treatment and recovering from it. I visited him twice during those days, and we had tremendous times of conversation and prayer. I carried resources like books and magazines to read and to encourage his heart for the battle.

The trust won and the relationship developed were surely a part of the newly open doors to work with Coach Irvin's team in the fall and winter. Being available and present in the moment of crisis gave me entrance for ministry with the coach, the other coaches and the players. I would encourage and even challenge you to walk confidently into hospital rooms and other places where we may encounter Serious Illness. It is more an opportunity to be embraced than an opponent to be avoided.

Ministry in Moments of Crisis Being Fired

It's rather common in USA sport, and I'm sure around the globe, to hear of a coach of a team or a manager of a club being fired by the university or ownership of the club. Most of the coaches I know do their best to be philosophical about the situation and to says that it's a part of the business. They act like that takes the sting out of the process, but I know there is more going on than what they will easily acknowledge.

Having experienced the loss of a job, I know bitterly the feelings of failure, separation and even shame which accompany the unwilling termination of one's employment. Even when the coach shows the strong face and confident posture, in his heart there is a terribly personal loss which is felt deeply. In public, she may look fine, but in her quieter moments she's devastated.

It's much the same for the player who is cut from a team because of roster limits, for the team management professional who hears, "We need to go in another direction," and for the aging player whose salary and contract restrictions make him a more costly asset than the young, first year player.

In all these cases, the source of the pain is the grief of separation. Being fired is like a couple being divorced. The relationship is severed, it's often accompanied by emotional confrontation, accusations and raised voices. People on all sides of the broken relationship begin to take sides and to place blame on one or both parties. Eventually the open wounds heal over, but there are often unresolved and acrimonious attitudes left to fester under the skin. It's an ugly process and full of pain.

As I write, my mind is full of memories, mostly painful ones. I recall sitting over coffee with a coach who was about to negotiate her resignation, so she wouldn't be fired. I remember desperately trying to contact a coach who was fired and then avoided anyone associated with his former program, even those of us who loved him. He's still avoiding us. I can still hear the silence on the other end of a phone call when I called a recently fired Offensive Coordinator for a high profile college football team a few hundred miles from my home. All I could think to do was to offer my love and to pray for them over the phone. I was thrilled months later when I saw him, and he said that his family had kept my phone message for months and would periodically bring the whole family into the kitchen to listen to the "Roger call" as I prayed for them and their future.

The brutal truth is that most of us in sport find our worth in our performance and to be fired is the ultimate indictment of our worth to the team. It's as if the club is saying, "You are not worthy of being associated with us. You're no good. Go away." It cuts deeply into the fabric of our self-worth and gnaws at the soul.

As we serve the people of sport, we have surely encountered this in the past or we will certainly do so in the future. It is no less painful for us, if we care deeply for the people we serve. Our natural tendency will be to take offense for the coach (if we are strongly attached) or to run away from him (so as to not be tainted by the firing) or possibly even to be among those who pile on with the discontented fans ("I wonder what took so long? He was terrible."). We would be wise to do none of the above. Just like when my friends get divorced, I simply refuse to take sides and seek to love everyone involved. Those separated by the firing are not just the coach and her team, but everyone on the coaching staff, the support staff including physios, equipment managers, office personnel, media and more. We must pursue our relationships with all of the above in extravagant love and understanding.

Ministry in
Moments of Crisis Death

Death is terribly final. It crushes those who love the one who is dying and robs them of precious communication with the one they love. In November of 2010, I was holding my mother-in-law's hand as she labored for her final breaths. I felt her pulse ebb from regular and strong, to irregular, to faint and then to finally cease altogether. I watched as the finality of her passing brought on still another stage of grief for her husband, children, grandchildren and friends.

We who serve people in the world of sport are equally subject to Death and its crushing effects as anyone else. Most of the people with whom we work, however are often of the mind that they are bulletproof and never give a conscious thought to the inevitability of death and dying. In university settings we work with young people eighteen to twenty-two years of age who feel like they're invincible. Death seems even more remote than responsibility or the consequences of sin. Many are suddenly confronted with Death's wicked cheap shots when a coach, teammate, parent or a sibling dies in a car crash, after suffering a heart attack, as the victim of violence or even due to suicide. Each brings its own special, rancid smell of pain and loss.

Just two days before my family's loss this fall, our Head Baseball Coach died. He had battled a rare form of cancer for several years, but that horrible disease doesn't play fair, and it ultimately overtook him. To quote George Bernard Shaw, "Death is the ultimate statistic. One out of one dies." I was privileged to spend some time with Coach Cal's widow the day he died and to also break the news to his team in the locker room. Thirty young, strong, fit and seemingly death-proof men were suddenly thrust into the crucible of Death and its equally brutal twin, Grief. The coaching staff was overcome with emotion and felt ill equipped to handle the situation. I was glad to contribute to the process of grieving and healing for the team and the staff.

As we serve sportspeople, we may occasionally be called upon to assist in these matters. We would do well to prepare through reading the Scriptures and taking note of how our Lord handled grief, death and mourning. We would do well to read other books and journals for tips for helping people understand their feelings and the process they will encounter due to the loss of their friend, teammate or family member.

May I challenge you to walk confidently into these moments of grief? Let's carry the same attitude as our Lord as we make our way to funeral wakes, to graveside services and to private meetings with grieving families. Let's love as extravagantly as Jesus did at Lazarus' grave, and let's carry hope and faith into often despair filled rooms.

Ministry in Moments of Crisis
Community Tragedy

When a community is shaken by tragedy it stamps the moment on their individual and collective memories, awakens many souls to their mortality and creates a momentarily open door for effective ministry.

One need only mention Marshall Football or September 11, 2001, and memories come flooding to our consciousness related to tragedy. Some of us can remember plane crashes, like Marshall University's Football team in 1970, involving Wichita State University Football also in 1970 and the University of Evansville Basketball in 1977. Those instances spread grief all across the region as well as among the communities from where each of their players had come to the universities.

In the last few years you may recall shootings on campuses like the one at Virginia Tech University and later at Northern Illinois University. I am familiar with sport chaplains and coaches at those schools and recall our conversations which were filled with grief and horror.

We all probably remember the circumstances peculiar to where we were on the morning of September 11 of 2001. I recall the shock, bewilderment and even a sense of denial that this could really be happening. Those feelings were soon replaced by a resolve to seek the Lord's best for people in the midst of this terrible tragedy. I recall many conversations with players and coaches as we all tried to make sense of the incident. Many had no room in their worldview for evil but had to rethink their positions. Many felt totally abandoned by God. Many others felt like God had let them and the USA down. The opportunity came simply because they were already thinking about God.

Rather than having simple, trite answers to all these complex issues, I worked to keep the conversations going and to point them to the Holy Scriptures for insight and comfort. In any sort of community tragedy, we are obviously ill-equipped to solve all the problems. We can, however, point them to an omnipotent, gracious, loving Savior for exactly what they need to live through this day and to get to the next one. If we coldly offer stock answers in the midst of community tragedy, it's like putting Band-Aids on a cancerous tumor. Such ministry is neither effective nor compassionate.

When community tragedy visits our world, let's be the ones who run toward the smoke and fire like the first responders on 9/11. Let's carry the life giving truth of Christ Jesus into the chaos, open wounds of emotion and even despair. Our presence will enlighten the path to hope, and our words will soothe weary souls.

Ministry in Emergency Rooms, Hospitals, and Surgery Centers

Across my years of serving sports teams I have had many occasions to visit emergency rooms, hospital rooms, and surgery centers with players, coaches, and administrators of the sporting community. While these are never pleasant occasions, they are regularly moments of the most profound and impactful ministry. I'd like to offer some observations from those visits and some tips for how to approach them, as they will certainly come to you as well.

One never feels competent when walking into an emergency room, hospital, or surgery center. Every time I approach the front door of one of these facilities I feel inadequate. I wonder what I have to offer. I wonder about what I am about to encounter. I wonder if I'll be able to handle the gravity of the moment and the potential emotional flood that awaits me. Every time, I stop, pray, and keep walking. This is not about me, nor my training, nor my ability to empathize, nor my ability to console, it's about being Christ Jesus' presence in a time of crisis. The Lord invariably carries me along in each situation, to my utter amazement.

Care for the people, respect the medical personnel, listen to the hearts. Early on in my experience I felt compelled to have the right words to say, but of late I seldom have anything to say. There are no magic words to make everything okay. A much better approach is to ask questions to open their hearts and to help them deal with their fears, questions, and worries. Treat the medical personnel, nurses, technicians, administrators, and doctors, with respect and understand your boundaries. Ask permission to go to more secure places in serving the patient, his or her family, and significant others. I have been allowed into intensive care units, maternity rooms, surgery prep rooms, recovery rooms, and other locations that are highly privileged spots because I treated the personnel with respect and earned their trust over time. Ask good questions, speak in low tones, respect privacy, and look people in the eye. Their hearts will open widely to you.

Bring a resource for their encouragement. The coming hours and days are likely to have a lot of time to read as their normal life of activity is interrupted by bed rest, doctor visits, waiting for appointments, and weeks of recovery. I often bring a devotional book, a book of prayers, or simply a card written with encouraging words and scriptures. I will fold down the corners of pages of the devotions that could have particular relevance to one recovering from injury, or I'll put Post It notes in pages of a prayer book to catch the attention of those being served. Long after we have left their presence, these resources speak to their hearts and enable them to connect with the Lord in their most desperate hours.

Offer to pray, privately. When I am with a patient and his or her family, I watch for the most appropriate moment to pray with them. As I am chatting with the people, I am listening for their hearts to open. I am seeking a moment with sufficient privacy to lean in, to offer to pray, to take a hand or to touch the injured shoulder, knee, or ankle, and to lift a quiet, intense, and unashamed prayer for the Lord's healing power to move in my friend's life. I pray for the immediate concern, for the patient's anxiety, for the doctor's skill, for quick and complete recovery, and for restoration to the sport they love. Above all, I pray for the Lord to accomplish His purposes in this person's life.

Leave with encouragement and an invitation to stay connected. I don't normally stay throughout the entire surgery, nor a long time in a hospital visit. Staying too long usually becomes awkward and ends poorly. After we have chatted, connected well, and prayed together, I am usually headed for the door. I will leave my card and an invitation to stay connected by phone or text message. I say, "I'll see you at practice. Let me know if I can serve you in any way. I'll look forward to your return to the team." This visit is simply one step in the long process of relationship development, but it is an important one. Make the best of this opportunity and then watch for the next one.

As I have been writing, a number of situations have flashed through my mind. Many of them have been instrumental in the development of relationships with coaches, competitors, doctors, nurses, and even administrators. I pray that your service is also graced by the beautifully intimidating experience of ministry in hospital rooms, ERs, surgery waiting rooms, and even hospice situations. The Lord Jesus walks into those moments with us, carries us along in His purposes, and accomplishes His will through us.

How to Finish:

Why do competitors leave their sport?

What are the reasons for the disappearance of people who love sport and have lived in sport for most of their lifetimes? There are a number of factors which lead to the end of one's sporting career, many of them are listed and discussed below.

One's eligibility expires—this happens mostly in collegiate sports in the USA. A player has four years of eligibility to compete in college sports across a span of five years. Occasionally an injury or some other issue may extend that to six years but it's the rare exception. Most competitors can see this coming for at least a year, but some don't really grasp it until they're about to compete in the last game or meet of their careers. This factor ends the vast majority of collegiate sportspeople's competitive sports careers.

Loss of opportunity—this happens in many sports, even to the most talented and host highly achieving, simply due to the lack of professional sports opportunities. There is no professional swimming tour, no pro Greco-Roman wrestling league, nothing beyond the amateur ranks for field hockey, cross country and most other sports. The loss of opportunity leads to the competitor's withdrawal from daily training, from regular competition and leads many to transition their participation to recreation or to a complete cessation of everything sport related.

Other responsibilities—Family, career and other matters suddenly consume the competitor's time and priorities. Competitors who had previously trained dozens of hours per week have their lives of practice, conditioning and competition in sport replaced by a similar number of hours devoted to study, preparation, meetings, travel and family time. Their lifestyle in sport is squeezed out by the limited number of hours in a day and a new devotion to other priorities and responsibilities.

One is expelled from sport—this happens more than we'd like to say and for a wide number of reasons. Drug use, violence, academic failure, theft, cheating, poor performance and other matters can lead to the competitor's ejection from their place in sport. It usually takes a string of bad decisions, many instances of foolish behavior or consistently poor athletic performances for one to be kicked to the curb. Most coaches and most sports organizations seem to give the competitor every opportunity possible to recover and to stay with the team, but in many instances, it's just not enough.

One is injured—the sports landscape is littered with the torn cartilage and strained ligaments of sportspeople. I've occasionally been a part of conversations with competitors who have been confronted with the grim reality that their bodies will no longer support their love for the sport and the knowledge that continuing to train and to compete likely jeopardizes their long-term health and mobility. These are painful talks as their passion for the sport and their desire to compete is seldom worn out before their bodies are.

Conflicts with a Coach—sadly this happens all too often.

Competitors and their coaches often disagree about playing time, training issues, team rules and even culture issues within a team, organization or club. Occasionally these matters can't be resolved, and a power struggle ensues. More often than not, the coach wins, and the competitor finds himself with nowhere to compete. Suddenly, she's on the outside of sport looking in.

Loss of interest—in my observation across many years of working with collegiate athletes in various sports, this happens often among junior and senior sportspeople. After two or three years in the sport at this level, one can see if he or she is able to compete strongly. If so, he or she stays engaged, trains hard and remains committed to the sport, to goals and to the team. If not, it's very common for the competitor to lose interest, to become laxer related to training, diet, sleep and other disciplines. In some cases the player feels trapped because his or her tuition is covered by a scholarship and to withdraw means the loss of financial aid. Their loss of interest comes at a high price, both emotionally and financially. The loss of interest leads to sport becoming very mundane, passionless and even painful.

Retirement Whether at age fifteen or fifty, many sportspeople reach the end of their sports careers and finish with joy and satisfaction. This is the best-case scenario. Any of the factors listed above can lead to one's retirement from sport, but if one has the presence of mind and the freedom of heart, he or she can embrace the end of a sporting career with a smile. If one understands that he is not defined solely by his role on the team or his participation in the sport, he can release the sport and move into the next chapter of his life with a clear mind and a contented heart.

As we serve the men and women of sport, we must help them realize that their identity is not to be found solely in their sporting lives. Sport itself and society in general will drive them toward that, but we are responsible to remind them of their identity in Christ Jesus. Before the foundation of the world He chose them to be His. From the day their birth He was seeking relationship with them. In every moment of their lives, on and off the field of competition, He has been speaking to their hearts. Upon their passing from this life, He will receive them into His presence. The sportsperson's identity is in Christ, from their earliest experiences with the sport and certainly on the day of their exit from the sporting life. (Ephesians 2:10)

Let's be faithful to walk beside those who leave sport, for whatever reason, to love extravagantly, to serve selflessly, to counsel and to remind them of their infinite value in the eyes of our Lord.

Serving Those Near the End of Their Careers

In the lives of every competitor and coach we serve there is one inevitable event, the end of his or her career. At some point, he or she has played the final game, run the final race, swam the last lap, hit the final shot, had the final at bat, inning, quarter, or period of his or her competitive career. While some who compete in sport may go on to be a coach, even that career will run its course, and suddenly the weight of that moment is felt again.

Many of those we serve make this transition very well and rather easily. They are usually the ones who derive very little of their personal identity from their sporting life. The ones who are at most risk in this moment are those whose lives in sport fully consume all that they are. Some see the final day coming from a long way off and begin to prepare for it. Others find themselves overwhelmed by the gravity of the moment as they change clothes in the locker room immediately after the final competition.

Across twenty-five seasons of collegiate and professional sport I have witnessed a broad range of emotions in these moments. Some finish with a sigh (as Moses describes in Psalm 90), they are simply spent and are relieved at the finality of their careers. Some finish in a flood of tears as this era of their lives is over and they feel it as grief, though a part of them has died. Others become bitter and look back on their investment of time, energy, emotion, relationships, injury, and pain as a net loss rather than a gain. Still others seem to glide through the day without apparent difficulty, but a couple of weeks later they are stunned at the sudden appearance of free time and leisure.

One of our men's swimmers from a few years ago shared his thoughts with our FCA group one evening. Although we had been talking about the end of career issues for a couple of years, he said it still hammered his heart and mind after he touched the wall for the final time at the end of his unsuccessful attempt to qualify for the USA Swimming Team for the 2012 Olympic Games. "It's like I had been writing right-handed for my whole life, and then suddenly I had to start writing left-handed." That is how he described the depth of the change in lifestyle he experienced.

A coaching friend of mine recently retired due to health concerns. It was the most difficult thing he had ever done as the passion for the game and the daily process was still there, but it appeared it could also kill him. "I've never done anything else." He was looking straight down the barrel of a crippling loss of identity and wondered who he would be if he didn't wear the title "Coach."

Given the power of this epoch in one's sporting life and the fact that it will come to everyone at some point, I would like to offer some strategies to help those you serve navigate these turbulent waters safely and successfully.

• Help them see the end of career issues before they arrive. Ask questions about their plans for post-career life. Talk about family, calling, life purpose, short-term and long-term plans.

• Encourage them to journal during the last season of

their careers and to thereby capture each day's memories, moments of significance, joy, and sorrow.

• Ask them to share their stories of career highlights, funny moments, times of joy and fulfillment. Ask about the most significant people and situations in their sporting lives.

• Discuss how their lives in sport uniquely qualify them to serve, to lead, and to make significant contributions beyond sport.

• Help them see that they are of infinite value to you, to others, and ultimately to God, in or out of sport.

• Help them to find their identity in a vibrant, living relationship with Christ Jesus. They are infinitely loved and identified with Christ, even more than as a competitor or coach.

Your presence in walking with them, your wisdom in guiding their approach, and your kindness in understanding their hearts will go a long way in assisting your sporting friends to make the painful transition from sporting life to that of "former coach or competitor."

Dealing With Coaching Staff Transitions

Every year in sport there are dozens of changes among head coaching positions, multiplied by their staff's transitions. This displaces hundreds of coaches and their families each year. We can serve them by understanding the situation and positioning ourselves for effective ministry.

Related to the outgoing staff:

· If the staff was fired, understand that this feels like failure and a lot like death to them.

· Help the coaches to see this situation within the sovereignty of God. The Lord is not surprised by this.

· Understand that the transition is probably harder on the coach's family than on the coach.

· Be available to them. They may not want much company, but if they welcome your presence, be there.

· Be prepared for the termination of some relationships. Some relationships will live beyond their tenure with your team, but others will cut off all ties to this place, and you could be cut off as well.

· Communicate respect and thankfulness for their time with your team as well as hope for their future.

· Assure them of your prayers and availability to serve.

· Written communication is very good and can be an enduring encouragement to them. Send a card, an email and/or periodic text messages to stay in touch with them.

Related to the incoming staff:

· Pray for favor with the athletic administration and the

new head coach.

· When a new head coach is announced, send a letter of congratulations immediately (keep it to one page).

· When the coach is settled into the office, get an appointment to welcome him/her and to offer your assistance.

· Bring a gift (a book) that is reflective of your desired relationship with the coaching staff and team.

· A wise attitude is reflected in offering to do "as much or as little as the head coach believes appropriate."

· When discussing a role with the team one can reference his/her role with past coaching staffs, but don't lock into those methods or activities exclusively.

· Let the coach paint the parameters for your role and work to build trust and credibility from there.

· It is always wise to offer to serve with no strings attached. Guard your attitude from presumption.

· Come prepared to discern the coach's perception of his/her, the staff and the team's needs.

When is it Time to Withdraw?

When is it time to withdraw? How does one know when it's the right time to resign his or her role in serving sportspeople? This is likely the most painful part of our tenure of service because of the tearing it does at the fabric of our hearts. When we serve relationally, the loss of relationship hurts, and we feel the loss very personally. A USA colleague of mine was recently released from his role with a prominent university, and it was very painful to him. He is seeking his next station of service, and I am certain he will land on his feet, but neither his, my, your, nor my opportunities last forever.

Below are some thoughts about factors that may make it time to withdraw from your service as a sports chaplain, character coach, or sports mentor.

When your opportunity evaporates Whether due to coaching changes, management or administration decisions, or other factors, it's pretty common that one's opportunity to serve a team or club could simply evaporate. This has happened to me at least twice over the years. In each case I approached the new coaching staff properly, offered to serve, but the offer was declined. Suddenly the opportunity was gone. It was time to seek new opportunity, and it has appeared each time.

When you lose your passion for the people and the process The moment that I find that I am more annoyed with the people of a particular team than I am energized by them, it will be time to leave this role to another person. When I begin to dread visits to the practice field, the court, the pool, the track, or the ballpark, it is time to get out. When I can no longer handle long bus rides, hours at practices, the alternating elation of victory and crushing pain of loss, it will be time to leave.

When you sense God's calling to some other avenue of service It is altogether proper for one to serve in various ways, in differing capacities, with different communities across his or her lifetime. There are certainly seasons to sports culture, and there are seasons to one's service of Christ. Observe Jesus' ministry in the Gospels. His areas of service varied widely as the geography changed, and the people groups he encountered changed. He did not hang out at Jacob's well throughout his ministry, just during John chapter 4. He was in Galilee for a season, in Jerusalem frequently, east of the Jordan on occasion, and even venturing through Samaria. We may find the Lord leading our hearts to a new station in our service. If so, seek a way to transition wisely, leaving this opportunity to another who is called to serve.

When you can no longer fulfill the role's demands There will probably be a day when your body will no longer be able to handle the physical rigors that come with your role as a sports chaplain. The way I have chosen to serve requires a good deal of energy, walking, standing, and long periods of concentration. My way of serving is very physically demanding and at sixty-four years of age, I can still do it. What about at age seventy? What about beyond that? If I cannot change how I serve, and I can no longer meet the physical demands, it may be time to withdraw.

These are just a few of the factors that may inform our hearts that it is time to leave this avenue of service to another. I would ask you, as I ask myself, to evaluate your service at the conclusion of each season, to look forward to the next one, and to either commit completely to serving with abandon, or to wisely withdraw, enabling another to serve in your place.

The Apostle Paul challenges us in Ephesians 4:1 with these words, "I, therefore, the prisoner of the Lord, beseech you to walk worthy of the calling with which you were called..." I would echo his challenge by asking you to serve the people of sport with passion, energy, wisdom, and full commitment. That is service worthy of the calling with which we were called. Anything less is not worthy of Christ Jesus. When I can no longer do that, I will gladly walk away.

Appendix:
Resources and Links

These are links to various on-line resources. You may type the URL into your browser, or simply point your smart phone camera at the QR code and it will take you directly to the site. Each of them is searchable by topic, issue, etc.

Content developed by Roger Lipe:
Blog for Sports Chaplains and Character Coaches:
http://sportchaplainsportmentor.blogspot.com

Sports Chaplain / Character Coach Resources (Chapel talk outlines and Bible studies):
https://rlipe.blogspot.com

YouTube instructional videos for Sports Chaplains & Character Coaches:

https://www.youtube.com/playlist?list=PLBmz-pllyhtqx4olugj8CIOXwu0_oG7gV9

Prayer in Sport—model prayers for situations and people in sport:

http://prayerinsport.blogspot.com

Daily Devotions for Competitors:

http://devotions4competitors.blogspot.com/

Corazón de un Campeón—daily devotions for people of sport in Spanish:

http://corazondeuncampeon.blogspot.com

Biographical sketch of Roger D. Lipe:

http://rogerlipebio.blogspot.com

Links to other valuable resources for ministry in sport:

Cede Network Global Registry of Sports Chaplains:

https://chaplains.cedesports.org/login

Cede Network Resources:
    https://cedesports.org/network/resource-hub/

Global Sports Chaplaincy Association:
    https://sportschaplaincy.com/

Major Sports Events Chaplaincy:
    http://majorsportseventchaplaincy.org/

About the Author

Roger Lipe has served with the Fellowship of Christian Athletes in southern Illinois since 1994. He was born and raised in Carbondale, Illinois (USA) and currently resides there with his wife, Sharon. Their son, Jason, his wife Jenn, and granddaughters Addison and Elise are treasures to his soul.

Roger serves as chaplain or character coach to teams, coaches, and individual competitors at Southern Illinois University, and to the Southern Illinois Miners of the Frontier Professional Baseball League.

Roger is the author of fourteen books for ministry in sport. His global network of friends and colleagues has enabled him to make dozens of international trips to over twenty nations on five continents to facilitate the growth of sports chaplaincy.

About the Author